One Man's Incredible Journey to Save His Family and Country

NJ PEREZ - O PEREZ

First Edition

NEWMAN SPRINGS PUBLISHING
320 Broad Street
Red Bank, NJ 07701

First originally published by Newman Springs Publishing 2020

ISBN 978-1-64801-953-1 (Paperback)
ISBN 978-1-64801-954-8 (Digital)

Printed in the United States of America

Contents

Preface

The following novel presents the factual accounts, as informed by memory and the experience of having lived it, of the history of my family. Taking extreme measures when the bottom fell out from our society, we knew we had to do something. We were not heroes, but we found ourselves thrust into a Communist regime unexpectedly, and we could not abide living under Communist rule. Of course, with our actions, everything changed...our lives were thrown into instant chaos and near oblivion, *but our lives had changed already anyway due to our leader having lied to us about his persuasions.*

My message is a warning and is rather clear: *if it happened to us, it could happen to anybody...any family.* One day we were living our lives peacefully, attending to our children's needs, our home, our work—and the next day, darkness came and set up refuge in the hearts of our leaders, who before then seemed quite nice. Instead of a presiding good will in our country, we now had fear and death to watch over us. Rather than happy neighbors with whom we could share life's joys, we had block snitches who roused suspicion, intolerance, and paranoia. Please believe me and keep your guard up. World events change rapidly, and terrorism is the new normal for even so-called stable governments. Oh, the devil is strong, and his schemes fall right into the hands of nations who do not know, understand, or respect God.

Above all else, perhaps you may learn from our experience.

My life's history starts off like many others: an incredibly happy childhood spent growing up on a farm with loving parents and cousins, aunts, and uncles...good neighbors and friends, attending school and finding skills to use in the world, *and then blissful romance.* We all lived thankfully, not knowing just how dangerous the coming events stemming from our country's political turmoil would be. To be sure, we were quite aware of the political struggles within our government; however, it was the typical one side against the other that had gone on for decades, and we took it as being growing pains, and perhaps even a bit healthy and natural. *We vastly underestimated the dimensions of the factors of greed and the lust for power which ran beneath what we could see.* These two forces came together and elevated the struggle between the factions exponentially, and when this happened, all hell broke loose in a matter of days. It did not seem like hell at first, as we had a smiling political leader who was intelligent and charismatic, and who even presented a soft side with a seeming heart of gold.

How can you not trust that? Oh, we were foolish…wanting to believe the best. That is what I mean when I implore you to keep your guard up. What happened with astonishing speed right after those first few days still gives me nightmares. *So many were made to sacrifice their very lives, and the rest of us became directly and forever affected by the absolute madness which followed.*

I must here thank the members of my family who supported us, and my husband's colleagues, most who gave their lives for the mission about which you will read next. It was a miracle any of us survived at all, but it was those who lost their lives in service to ending Communism who deserve the ultimate credit for this story. Every person you will read about in the following pages had such hope, spirit, and courage, and they pulled together in order that we all might continue to pursue a life of freedom and away from tyranny. It is my intention to describe in the words which follow the dignity and honor of those who had lived the actual circumstances we had found ourselves embroiled. Since our world refuses to find peace and common ground, and some governments may endure while others fall, it is always the citizens who must become heroes. They and their loved ones are the ones who suffer most due to leaders who deny faith, have only their own interests to consider, *and who will stop at nothing to assure they remain in power.*

In these words, I hope to find a truth that eclipses all the suffering brought on by those lusting for power. Power-hungry and corrupt leaders do not communicate their intentions to their citizens because their hope is to ultimately control all thought via propaganda. Mass media is a powerful thing, but when used incorrectly, it causes mass hysteria and even cultural delusion. *However, when it is given the liberty to destroy truth, that is when our leaders get to influence citizens in wayward means. Since we cannot decide what we are told, we must remain diligent in what we believe; otherwise, what we hear when there is a lack of a neutralizing buffer can be absolutely erroneous.* I will do my best to tell the events as they truly had occurred, for facts themselves had been taken from us, *and we must never allow any dictator to squelch reality for all time.*

The following is a true story about how one family saw through the delusions and tried to change the course their country was taking. In order to protect people from the weight of the yoke handed to us by the devil, I have changed the names and some of the locations in order to shield those still living in the satanic hell Castro had created for the good citizens of my beautiful Cuba. Otherwise, the characters, events, and history presented in this novel are based on the true-life events of my husband's colleagues and our modest family. The author has used her own firsthand knowledge and experience and has researched extensively on some parts of the book which required factual historical perspective to add accuracy to the narrative.

Ultimately, I am hopeful that this book becomes a roadmap of how we all had better pay closer attention to current world affairs. No matter who we are or what ideology our leaders adhere to, there are many forces out in the world today which would very much like to take our property, our savings, our faith in God, and our very hope. These evil forces always seem to begin with the cry of the few who are disgruntled, feel they have been oppressed, and demand change. Many of these simply do not wish to have to apply themselves, and they would rather get their leaders to give them sustenance and shelter. *From there, it is always some other professional or leader, psychologist, or attorney who motivates them to fight for what is rightfully theirs.* They get others to hop on board, and their leaders soon demand a redistribution of wealth.

Then one morning, you wake up and find your husband on the run for his life, your property and possessions confiscated, and everybody is suddenly watching your every move. Wherever you are right now, however safe you may feel, remember, they call them changing times for a reason.

One political sidestep in the wrong direction is all that it takes.

Prologue

My grandparents came to Cuba from Spain decades ago, with the hope of working hard to establish themselves into a culturally rich community within the island province. It had taken them a lot of planning and hard work to get where they were when they had my parents, and likewise, my parents had set goals for themselves in order to make it the best life they could have for themselves, their family, their neighbors, and their community.

All four of my grandparents immigrated from Catalan, Spain, with their families when they were in their teenage years. Both my mom's and my dad's families lived in Santa Fe, Isle of Pines, Cuba, and that's where they met and formed their families. On my mom's side were my grandparents Ramon Julian Rodriguez and his beautiful wife, Antonia Rodriguez. On my dad's side were Alejandro Simon Gomez and Constanza Fernandez Gomez. They were farmers and marketeers. Insisting their children finish school, both families kept their children close to the farm.

My parents were Julian Benito Rodriguez and Catalina Rodriguez, two of the most notable youth in Santa Fe since they could dance like no other. They had known they were in love from early on when they met in secondary school. My grandparents, on both sides, often spoke about how often they would have to go out and parade around town as chaperones to the couple, who quickly became inseparable and who loved their long walks beneath the moonlight. They were the sparkle at dancing events around our community—at the town center and the outdoor fairs and events.

Santa Fe is a city on the Isle of Pines which is itself one of the beautiful islands just south of the western tip of the Cuban mainland. Isle of Pines is the second-largest Cuban island and the seventh-largest island in all of the West Indies. The island has a population of about eighty thousand citizens, and the capital and largest city is Nueva Gerona in the north. Santa Fe is its second largest and oldest city more toward the island's interior. Other communities surrounding it are Columbia, McKinley, Punta del Este, and Sierra de Casas. Much of the island is covered in pine forests, which is the source of the island's large lumber industry (and obviously, where we got our name). The northern region of the island is mostly low ridges, and from there, marble is quarried, while the southern region has a vast elevated plain. Besides lumber, agriculture and fishing are the island's main industries. Surrounding the island along its vast coast are black sand beaches formed by volcanic activity. The island itself is practically a great big pine forest with farms and estates sprinkled in for good measure. On the estates, agriculture crops such as tobacco, rice, and fruit crops are grown, and there is raising of stock.

Canary Islanders started arriving in late the 1500s and became the tobacco farmers of the region. Along with the protection of the pine forests, tobacco plantations and cattle ranches quickly sprang up due to the rich soil and open grazing land. Farmers who made a living from well-tended crops were colloquially named Guajiros, a native word that means, literally, *one of us.* By the mid-1800s, Europeans were hooked on the fragrant tobacco, and our island flourished. Sea routes opened for easier exporting of the crops. Santa Fe, like many areas of Cuba, had an influx of Asian laborers coming from the Philippine Islands to work on tobacco plantations.

A long highway connects the city to the capital Nueva Gerona, which is about twenty kilometers north and close to the northern coast of the island. Tree-lined streets and dazzling white brick and cement structures define Santa Fe. Most buildings have the popular columns rising from ground to roof in the historical Spanish architectural style, and wooden benches are plentiful beneath the trees, since the whole feeling of the town is about relaxing and enjoying the beautiful weather, the salty air, and the friendship of the community. The main transportation to and from the island is by boat or aircraft. On any given day, you can see many hydrofoils and motorized catamarans making the two- to three-hour journey back and forth from

Batabanó, on the coast of the mainland south of Havana, and Nueva Gerona. A much slower and larger cargo ferry takes around six hours to make the crossing but is cheaper. Unfortunately, the island's mild climate is also known for frequent hurricanes.

With its many beaches, Isle of Pines became a popular tourist destination back when I was in my twenties, and resorts soon started springing up across almost every area of its large coastline, with the most popular beach being Bibijagua Beach. Until the Cuban government expropriated all foreign-owned property in the early 1960s, much land along the coast had been owned by Americans, and the island contained a branch of the Hilton Hotels chain. That should be enough about the background of the island where we had lived.

I was born Angela Eulalia Rodriguez on August 19, 1927, at 2:00 a.m. I must admit that I had marvelous parents, and they gave me six siblings in total. I was the third to come along, and though some say I was very pretty, I saw myself as being a bit reserved and independent-minded, since I had a penchant for doing things my own way. Most would tell me later that I was not much of any trouble for my parents as an infant or toddler. As I grew, they reported to me that I was always very clean, organized, and quite fussy about putting things back in their place when I had finished using them.

My earliest memories take me back to the farm when I was about five, playing with my two oldest siblings Josephina, who would have been about eight, and who loved to be presentable no matter what the occasion, and Antonio, a year older than Josephina, who modeled himself as best as he could after our papo. At that time, I had two younger siblings, as well (the last two would come later)—Fernando, who was three years my junior, with big blue eyes, a dazzling shock of dark blondish hair, and who loved to eat; and finally Lilliana, who was only a toddler. Already, Lilliana enjoyed dressing up in fancy outfits.

Our mami, Catalina, was a seamstress who made dresses, and our papo, Julian, owned a lumber business and had his own distribution system with a fleet of six flatbed trucks. Eventually, two of my brothers would become drivers to transport the lumber to Nueva Gerona for processing and then transport to the mainland. In between their work, my parents and all the children helped look after the family farm which my mami's parents had started decades before. Mami's parents lived on the other side of the farm, and so we saw them frequently. They grew all sorts of vegetables: pumpkin, corn, peppers, and melons; and my mom's dad, my Grandfather Ramon, had done much business in years past with an American businessman named Mr. Smith. I remember Mr. Smith well since his accent was so peculiar to me. He always smiled at me and would regularly bring me a small trinket back from the states. Although he dealt mostly with Grandfather, he also came to the lumber yard occasionally to get things from Papo, who had learned a bit of English along the way so that he might be able to more clearly communicate with his American customers.

Due to his business arrangements, Grandfather Ramon, who I always called Papa Ramon, was quite knowledgeable about the best ways to make deals, and I would often ask him to teach me some of his best bargaining techniques, figuring someday I might need to know them. The farm also came complete with three large herds of cattle for milk, and we made our own cheese. On a more practical note, of course, we had plenty of meat for ourselves after the allotment Papa Ramon would set aside for public sale.

I would customarily spend the weekends with Papa Ramon and Abuela. My mami's two brothers, my Uncles Juan and Mateito, lived home with my grandparents since they did most of the hardest work on the farm. I loved them both, and the care they showed in helping a little girl around a large farm was wonderful. I loved the farm so much, with all of its activity and the animals, the fresh smells of crops growing after a heavy rainstorm, the wide open spaces, and plentiful places to go and find a spot for myself to read or play.

About a month before my seventh birthday, I was at my grandparent's house, and it was a Saturday morning. After waking up in the bedroom I called my second home, pushing off the fair, bright sheets of my bed, and watching the thin white linen window dressings ruffle to and fro in the wind, I stood up from my canopy bed and looked at all of my favorite toys lined up on the floor along the inside wall. I realized this was my dream bedroom, and that I loved it even more than my bedroom at home. With that pleasant thought in mind, I marched into the kitchen and immediately saw Grandfather sitting at the kitchen table, reading his daily newspaper.

"Papa Ramon, you must go and buy the flour today so I can make torta for everyone!" I exclaimed.

He glanced over the edge of the paper, a twinkling in his eyes. "Yes, yes, Angela, my sweet pumpkin, I have it on my list of things to do this morning after we get you washed up and dressed."

Abuela was fixing a plate of fresh eggs and the torta, which we had made yesterday, and so I sat at the table next to Papa Ramon. There was a glass of fresh squeezed orange juice set in my place, and so I took a sip and marveled at how sweet and refreshing it was. Papa Ramon was of medium height, broad-shouldered, and with a handsome face free of any whiskers. He had deep eyebrows which gave his expressions a bit more emphasis. Abuela was a beautiful woman, like Mami, though a bit older. She had long, light brown hair which came straight down to her shoulders, and her cheeks were smooth and rose-pink, but it was the sparkle in her hazel-colored eyes which made her stand out in appearance. At least, that is what I had always thought.

Abuela deposited a plate before me—the eggs stark white with a nice brown edge and a sunny yellow globe in each of their middles. "Angela, later, you will help me with the laundry out back in the sunshine. You can play for a bit once you get back with Papa Ramon, but then we must do our chores."

To me it was not a chore. I loved doing the laundry! Lifting my sleeves and using the washboard in the large metal bucket with the warm sudsy water sloshing around, and the clothes becoming cleaner with each swipe! *What could be finer?* I nodded and realized that this morning, there was also bacon, and the smell in the house was making my mouth water. Without further waiting, I next took a nice crispy piece of it into my fingers and chomped down. The torta had been toasted and slathered with butter, and I bit down on a piece. *Ummm...* sweet and buttery and salty all at the same time!

Abuela washed me, dressed me, and combed my fine hair, which was a glorious mixture of light brown, chestnut, and blond highlights. Everybody admired the coloring on top of my head. I did not know what I had done to get it but always enjoyed the interest just the same. I wore my pink dress with the yellow buttons down front and the red flowers printed into the fabric. Papa Ramon was wearing his regular business attire—black dress slacks and shoes, a light blue guayabera, and his brown fedora on top of his round head. He took his pipe, which, when lit, always smelled like fresh cherries. Holding my hand, we made a left at the end of the driveway and headed into town down the long, shady avenue which traversed town.

Along the way, we waved at neighbors who passed us in their cars and horse-drawn wagons. Some folks were walking, like us. Would you not know it? My best friend, Pilar, was just ahead of us, walking with her mami.

"Papa Ramon, let's catch up to them!" I insisted.

"I'm much too old and tired," he responded. When I looked up at him, I saw that he was smiling, joking with me as he would do. He snickered at me and then increased our pace. "C'mon, pumpkin. Let's do!"

When we had come just behind them, Pilar's mami turned and saw our approaching. "Well, look who it is! Good day to you, Ramon!"

"Mariana, how nice to see you on such a fine morning as it is!" Papa Ramon responded.

Pilar had turned and come to a stop. She smiled at us and then looked up at her mami. "Mami, can I go and play at Angela's house today?"

Her mami looked at Papa Ramon. "Well, we don't know if they are busy, darling. We'll have to see."

I looked up at my Papa Ramon, saying, "Well, once we get back, Abuela said I would have time to play before I have to help with doing the laundry."

He nodded at me and then turned and smiled at Pilar's mami. "I think we have our answer! We should be home in two hours, so why don't you plan on bringing Pilar by at about noon?"

With that, I had a play date scheduled for that Saturday.

The business district was crowded with shoppers. Papa Ramon knew almost everybody, and they all gave their regards, smiling and nodding back at us. Men sat at tables on the corners of the streets, laughing and playing dominos. There were several carts set up on the sidewalks selling various items of food. We came into the grocer's market, and it bustled with people. Right away, I smelled the familiar aroma of cheese and meat. We walked down several of the wide aisles looking over the goods, and Papa Ramon seemed very keenly aware of the prices being asked.

"Much too high," he would say every now and again.

He took a few things, carrying them in his arms. When we came to the flour, I watched him closely. He compared several brands and sizes of the bags. He looked down at me.

"Shall we get a small sack or a large sack?"

"A large sack," I said.

"Very well."

He took the large bag off the shelf, and we made our way to checkout. When it was our turn, Papa Ramon put the items down on the counter before the man behind the cash register.

"Vincent, your prices are getting much too high!" he exclaimed to the older gentlemen, who was going through our items and pressing buttons on the register.

The man, Vincent, had a gray mustache, was tall and thin, and wore a brown apron which extended across his chest and all the way to his ankles. "As are the prices I must pay for the goods in the first place!" Vincent snapped back at Papa Ramon.

"Then something is not right," Papa Ramon said. "We are producing the goods better than ever. Our fields are bringing great crops. What is going on? I'm telling you, something's not right!"

"Besides our newest politicians being crooks, just like the last ones were, I don't know of anything that is wrong, Ramon!"

"Okay, but keep your eyes open, will you? Try finding out what is causing the cost for the distribution and sale of goods to go higher and higher."

He gave Papa Ramon a stern look but nodded as he put our new belongings into a large brown bag.

We began our walk home, and it was getting hot already. As Papa Ramon took off his hat momentarily to wipe his forehead with his arm, I asked, "Why are prices of things going so high, Papa Ramon?"

"I have my suspicions, Pumpkin! Don't know for sure—but sometimes our leaders take more than their fair share from the people working hard to provide things that others need. The world has suffered from depression, which means that people could not make enough money to pay for those things we produced, and prices fell so much we did not make enough money *to keep producing those things,* like sugar, tobacco, fruit, and just about everything else. We got rid of one of our leaders, who was very bad for the people, and have just allowed another to take over. That is why I am upset to see prices of groceries going so high so quickly. We will see if our new leader does any better for his people, *meaning, all of us,* than the last one did."

It was why I loved Papa Ramon so—he treated me like an equal person even though I was young, and he did not keep things from me. He always respected my intelligence and allowed me to ask questions if I did not know what he had meant when he explained complicated things. I could understand most of what he had just said, if not everything, and as usual, it was his sentiment that I would intuit most clearly, thereby assisting the formulation of ideas and thoughts in my growing intellect.

When we arrived home, Pilar was already outside with Abuela, helping her tend to one of our small herb gardens which Abuela planted every year around the house. I ran over to help them.

"Help Pilar take those weeds from around the cilantro, Angela. Once you've completed that, you can go get your dolls and play by the swinging chair, and I will bring out some cold coconut water with lime for you both."

Abuela had gotten her knees dirty as she was on her hands and knees leaning into a tomato shrub trying to get all the weeds which had grown around the stalk. She never fussed about any of the burdensome things she had to do all day to keep the house, yard, and family running so well. Many times, I felt sorry for her because it seemed all she did was work and then more work. My mami had my sister and brother to help with everything needing to be done, but

Papa Ramon and Abuela's children were either grown and had moved away or were working all day on the farm.

Pilar and I washed in the basin outside the kitchen door and then ran inside to my bedroom. I always anticipated the look on her face when she would see my dolls all lined up on my bureau and some on the floor, ready for action.

"I just love this doll, Angela!" Pilar said as we came to the bureau.

She gently touched the top of Marissa's head. Marissa was the first doll I had ever made, with Abuela's help, using scraps of cloth and cotton stuffing, black hair made with painted strings, and bright red lips I had colored myself using a little paint Papa Ramon had found inside his toolshed.

"She's just so beautiful and soft."

"You can pick her up, Pilar!" I said.

Pilar took her into her arms like she was gently holding a newborn baby. She began rocking her, and I smiled.

"She loves that."

I took the doll that had been sitting quietly next to Marissa, my second homemade doll which I had named Isabel, who was Marissa's younger sister, and held her gently in my arms. Isabel was pretty, like Marissa, but smaller. She also wore a yellow dress, whereas Marissa wore dungarees and a flannel shirt.

Speaking in a high-pitched faux voice, I lifted Isabel toward Marissa and said, "C'mon, Marissa, let's go out and play by the swing with our friends!"

Pilar used her squeaky voice to try out a voice which Marissa might have. "Okay, let's go! We can drink coconut water with lime and sit in the grass watching the kids playing!"

I grabbed my doll amenities such as cups and a pitcher, then some of my other dolls, most of them store-bought and given to me by Mami and Papo, aunts and uncles, and of course, Abuela and Papa Ramon; and we headed back out the kitchen door. We got set up and sat in the grass and began to play. Abuela brought us our drinks, which we happily shared with our dolls. Watching Pilar playing, I realized she and I had so much in common and that we both enjoyed the traditional things and routines of life. We would almost always agree what would come next in our playtime, and there was usually very little conflict between us. I loved Pilar so much. Her parents were farmers, like Papa Ramon and Abuela. Eventually, Pilar's mami came for her, and I put my dolls away safely in the comfort of my bedroom.

Abuela was in the kitchen waiting for me when I was through. "C'mon, Angela darling, time for laundry."

"Yes, ma'am!"

I immediately followed her out back to the two large, rectangular tables in the small courtyard which contained a pit for barbequing meat, wooden chairs, and a couple of benches with smaller tables beside them. Abuela had already poured hot water from the large, black iron pot in the kitchen into the two wash bins. The dirty clothes had all been neatly stacked in three piles behind the wash bins, and a small stool had been set up in front of the table by the wash bin I was to use.

Abuela poured powdered soap from a box into both bins and said, "Start with that pile, Angela. Remember, do a thorough job!"

I grabbed one of Uncle Juan's beige guayaberas and dunked it into the warm water. Swishing it around in the water before bringing it up along the rippled metal of the washboard, I then firmly held it while scrubbing it up and down with as much force as my hand would permit. I tried liquifying any of the soap granules which had not dissolved in the water by catching them between the fabric of the shirt and the metal. It was so hot today, and yet each day of the summer would attain a temperature that at some point made one just want to lie down and fall asleep. I felt sweat forming on my forehead, but I knew that doing these chores was all a part of living, and so they must be done. Abuela would sweat just from being outdoors on a day like today, and so I never complained about the heat.

As she did her own washing, I know Abuela was keeping a careful eye on my work. Occasionally, I would look up at her, and she would nod approvingly. We put all the clean clothes into another basin, and these we would have to wring out once we were finished scrubbing each article of clothing in today's three piles. The muscles in my right arm and back began aching, but I continued as diligently as I had started. I always wanted Abuela to approve of the work I did.

"You are going to be a strong woman someday, my angel!" Abuela said as we continued washing clothes. "You will make some man a great wife, with children of your own who will love you endlessly."

I smiled but offered no other response. It seemed so far off as to not even warrant a discussion. As soon as we were done with laundry, I took my nap. Fresh sea breezes coming through the window helped keep me cool, even though the linen sheers were a distraction at first, as they ruffled continuously in the air. Exhausted, I soon fell asleep and rested peacefully. When I awoke, it was already late afternoon, and Papa Ramon was ready to make tortas.

He took down the measuring cup from the cabinet above the counter and handed it to me. Carefully, I scooped it down into the sack of flour which we had purchased earlier and brought out a full cup. Papa Ramon began to heat the pan on the stove as I added to the flour, first salt, then baking soda, and finally my secret ingredient, *sugar.* I do not know where I got this idea from still today. Perhaps it was a mistake at first, thinking about the biscuits and other breads Mami would make which required some sugar to help the yeast to grow. Or maybe I thought all tortas had sugar in them. Whatever it was, I had started adding it to the flour every time I made tortas with Mami, Abuela, or Papa Ramon, and they all greatly enjoyed the variation. With Papa Ramon peering over my shoulder, I mixed all the ingredients together with my hands and then slowly added water to the mixture. My hands became gooey as I blended the water into the dry ingredients. Mami had taught me that just the right amount of water was crucial to good tortas. And so, I always started with less than what I would need in total and then added just a few drops a little at a time until the dough was perfect—workable and yet not too soft. Soon I had a perfect dough, and knowing how much effort I gave to get it just right, Papa Ramon looked down at me with a huge grin.

He helped me to roll out balls which we then flattened with our palms and fingertips. With lard in the pan, we began cooking the bread. Just when the top of each piece had made bubbles which then dried and became firm, we turned over our cakes. Flipping them, we saw the cooked side had both firm white and tan parts intermingled with raised ripples of charred and black crust. *Just how they were meant to be!* We split the first one in half to test it, and Papa Ramon and I tasted. They were perfect! Firm outside and soft inside, with an earthy taste that was just a bit sweet. Abuela came over to snatch the second one, and then Uncle Juan, having just bathed after a long day on the farm, got the third. He smiled and winked at me.

"Perfect, as usual," he said, plopping the entire rest of the torta into his mouth after taking first bite.

I put the fourth aside for Uncle Mateito, who had gone to the market and would be home shortly. When finished, we had only six left over for breakfast in the morning.

Papa Ramon said, "Tomorrow, before church, we will make another batch before you leave us to go home until next weekend!"

I nodded and had a great big smile, and it made me feel important knowing that my work was so cherished.

On Monday morning, I was home with Mami, in my bedroom playing with my dolls with my brother Fernando. Lilliana was asleep in the crib as Mami was sweeping out the entire house. Our house was a bit larger than Abuela and Papa Ramon's, and altogether we had four bedrooms, a utility room, two bathing rooms, a large kitchen and dining area, and a television set in the living room. Josephina and Antonio had gone with Papo to help in the office at the lumberyard today. Mami said she would be making rice, black beans, and grilled chicken for supper tonight, one of my favorite meals. Today she was wearing her long gray skirt and a white blouse, which I thought made her face even that much prettier. Mami was beautiful even when she was doing housework, and she always hummed a song while engaged in doing any of the numerous chores necessary taking care of her family. Her skin was silky and cream-colored, and she had long flowing light-brown hair with auburn highlights, which she mostly kept in a bun on top of her head. When she and Papo went out to a dinner engagement, Mami allowed her hair to come down, and its elegance could never be overstated.

Papo, on the other hand, wore a large mustache and had a sharp jawline which gave him character. He was tall and thin and had an easy smile most of the time. Mami would say that he had an imposing presence when he was at work or when dealing with business matters of any kind. His intelligence on a variety of matters is what brought other men to seek his opinion on any number of subjects. *To me, he was just Papo*—loving, kind, affectionate, and full of information whenever I needed answers about most anything.

My younger brother Fernando was often called *angelic* because with his perfect face, shocks of blond hair, and bright blue eyes, he often made everybody smile with his presence alone. He had a great sense of humor even at his young age, and because of this, I enjoyed making him smile and laugh, as it was quite easy to do. Whenever I brought my dolls to life with variations of my voice, and then created situations wherein they were part of a family doing family events together, he would be endlessly entertained watching my dolls enact the various scenarios which I invented. This morning, Marissa was chastising Isabel for having borrowed one of her dresses and getting it mucked up with dirt from the garden. Upset, of course, Isabel began bawling loudly, getting the attention of their Mami and Papo. The two dolls playing the part of Mami and Papo were given to me last year by Papa Ramon for my birthday, and they were very sophisticated in their appearance and range of movement. The male doll had a mustache and wore a black hat, while the female doll looked more like a glamourous entertainer rather than someone's mami. Nonetheless, I invested a great deal of energy into their being believable parents to my homemade little girls.

"Go to your room!" the mami yelled at Marissa in a firm voice for having made Isabel so upset.

Marissa complained in a high-pitched squeal, "But, Mami, she ruined my dress!" Marissa pointed at Isabel with a steady, if not a bit stiff, fist.

By this time, the papo had all he could take. He shook side-to-side with anger as he yelled at them in a very deep voice, "Quiet, all of you! I will not have such a racket in my home!"

When I looked away from my puppets to catch a glimpse of my little brother, Fernando was rolling uncontrollably in spasms of giggles on the floor. Mami had to even stick her head into my bedroom to make sure he was simply laughing and not otherwise ill or upset. I know she enjoyed the fact that I could keep my little brother entertained during the day. He was adorable, and it was almost always a pleasure for me to do it.

Later, we both helped Mami to begin preparing dinner. Mostly, I had to keep Fernando occupied again as he was more curious than helpful. However, I was able to help measure the beans and then season the avocado we would be having as a side dish.

After our nap, before dinner, I played outside by myself amongst the flowers and small trees next to our large garden in the backyard. I always looked forward to a little bit of time for myself each afternoon, even if I did nothing more than walk around the yard while singing or humming. When I saw Papo drive up in his small truck, I ran to the driveway to greet my older siblings and Papo.

"Hello, darling!" Papo said to me as he got out of the truck. He leaned down and kissed me on top of the head and then brought out something from his pocket. "This is for you!" He opened his palm, and I saw it was a piece of red candy in a wrapper. "Mr. Smith came by today and missed you."

Surprised, I looked up. "Why did he come to the lumberyard and not to the farm for Papa Ramon?"

Papo smiled. "Because today, he just so happened to need my lumber and not fruits and vegetables!"

I smiled and took the candy from Papo's palm.

"It's cherry," he said.

"We have a whole box of it," my sister Josephina said, holding up a small white box of candy. She was always quite presentable and pretty. Today, she had worn her bright yellow skirt and pink blouse.

"But Papo said we can't have any more until after dinner," Antonio added, coming around the truck to stand before me. Tall and thin like Papo, nobody would have any doubt that he was Papo's son.

"But you may have the piece I have given you now since your brother and sister already had one piece earlier," Papo exclaimed, at which point, I eagerly unwrapped my candy and plopped it into my mouth. It took a moment to get the full flavor. Soon, I realized that it was the most succulent taste of cherry I had ever experienced. Somehow, it was tart and sweet at the same time, and it made my mouth both water and pucker as I let it dissolve in my mouth without chewing it.

Together, we all walked into the house, whereupon I told Mami all about the candy. She responded by saying she could not wait until after dinner to try a piece. Papo and my siblings washed up, and then we all came together at the kitchen table. Mami had put all the dishes on the table, and it looked and smelled wonderful. We ate with gusto as Papo shared how well my brother and sister did at the office with filing bills and invoices, cleaning, dusting, and watching him manage his workers and customers throughout the day. Mami informed that I had been quite a help with preparing the meal and keeping little Fernando busy all day.

After we had eaten, Josephina and I helped Mami wash the dishes and put things away. A few minutes later, Antonio came rushing back into the kitchen. "Josephina, where is the box of cherry candies? I wanted Mami to try one, and I can't find it."

Papo, who was still sitting at the table reading the morning paper, looked over the top of the newspaper toward the kitchen counter.

Josephina answered, "I put it right on the counter over there by the cookie jar."

Antonio pushed several jars around, looking behind them. He opened some of the cabinets and shuffled through various items within them.

Papo said, "Yes, I remember seeing it right there at the end of the counter right before we started to eat."

"It's nowhere!" Antonio exclaimed, perplexed.

Josephina finished drying her hands on a kitchen towel and came to where Antonio was. She began searching the same area he just had, but I noticed she was not looking very hard. "Mami, did you see the box of candies? It was a white box about the size of a large bar of soap."

Mami shook her head and began looking at the other end of the counter. Papo even got up and began looking about. He searched the living room, and Josephina went and investigated one of the washrooms. Antonio looked throughout the living room as well.

I could not believe it had gone missing. After all, it was I who had told Mami just how delicious the candies were, and I knew she had looked forward to trying one. Instead of searching, I put my mind on to the task. Everybody had looked in all of the apparent places the box could be, and so I figured it must be somewhere else somehow, somewhere least expected. That is, of course, unless a hungry ghost had come along unexpectedly. I tried to recall Josephina's steps once we had come into the house from the truck earlier. It was then that I realized that Josephina was now wearing different clothes than she had on throughout the day. Immediately, I went to her bedroom and to the dirty clothes bin next to her closet. Right on top of the pile was her yellow skirt. I lifted it up and could feel something large in her pocket, and I knew at once I had hit pay dirt. I fumbled in the pocket of her skirt, and my hand soon wrapped around the box of candies.

I immediately ran into the kitchen. "I found it!"

Papo was thrilled. He came running to me and took the box from my hand. "Angela found it!" he exclaimed to the others. Everybody hurried back into the kitchen, and I was called upon to explain the process of my discernment.

After explaining how I had noticed that Josephina had changed clothes, my oldest sister interrupted me. "Yes, now I remember! I had put the box on the counter originally, but then I went to wash and change before dinner." Her cheeks became flush with embarrassment. "I wanted one more piece...*they were so good*, and so I snuck the box into my bedroom to take out another piece and then forgot I had put the box in my pocket! I convinced myself I had returned it to the counter!"

Everyone shook their heads but smiled doing so.

Papo said, "Good thing we had Angela's sound logic or else we might not have found the candy until they were soaking in detergent water, melting at the bottom of the wash bin!"

Mami looked at me like I had created a miracle, and I knew instantly that I loved this kind of attention. This would be the beginning of my reputation as a finder of all missing things (which I would nudge along purposefully just a few days later, as you are about to read). Mami finally took a piece of the candy and then handed me a piece as well. A moment later, her face erupted in joy as she left it to dissolve in her mouth. She loved it and had another, and then so did everyone else, including Fernando, who made quite a face when the candy first started dissolving.

So now, coming back to how I helped to secure my reputation as finder of lost objects; three days after this, on Thursday morning, I implemented a plan which had taken all of Wednesday afternoon for me to concoct. I have never told a soul about this until now, and even so, I still feel quite embarrassed and a bit ashamed of my behavior.

Papo would always put the keys to his truck on the small table in the hallway by the front door of the house, right next to the vase where Mami placed fresh flowers from the garden every day. They are there from the moment he comes home each evening until the moment he leaves for work the next morning. I waited Wednesday night until I knew everybody had gone to bed. Then I snuck out of my own. If I were to be caught, I would simply say I had to use the toilet. Tippy-toeing down the hallway as quiet as a mouse, I retrieved Papo's keys. I had cleverly thought about where to put them—and now I snuck into the living room and put them beneath the cushion of Papo's favorite chair. Making sure everything else looked exactly as it had before they retired for the day, I snuck back into bed and could not wait for morning to arrive.

I awoke as the sun was rising, which was quite early for me. Papo would be leaving in about an hour, and I listened as he shaved in the bathroom and then tried to quietly get dressed in their bedroom so as not to awaken us younger children. I heard Mami making breakfast, and finally, when Papo kissed Mami goodbye for the day, I got out of bed once again. I rushed to the bedroom door and watched Papo as he went to the hallway table for his keys. I saw the look of shock on his face when he realized they were not there. He patted his pockets with both hands, with no success (of course). He went back into the kitchen and asked Mami if she had seen his keys. She said no and that is when he began a frantic search for them. Papo hated being late to the lumberyard. After a few moments more, I finally sprang into action.

"What's the matter, Papo?"

"My keys, Angela, my keys are missing. They are always here, on this hallway table, but today they are not. Help us to search for them, sugar, will you?"

"Yes, Papo, of course."

I crawled beneath the table in the hallway, then went into the kitchen and scampered beneath that one. I moved the cookie jar and all the other jars and containers on the kitchen counter. I rushed into the bathrooms and all the bedrooms, then the utility room, and finally I came into the living room. Papo was in there searching the large table where he kept his liquors, and Mami was looking beneath newspapers on the credenza. Without pause, I made my way to Papo's chair. I lifted the cushion and was thankful they were right there where I had put them.

"I found them!" I shouted.

Papo, once again, came running to me. He took the keys in one hand and then hugged me firmly with the other. "Once again, my sweet Angela has saved the day!" Papo said. He was so happy, he pinched me gently on my cheek. "She will be forever known as Angela, *finder of lost valuables!*"

Chapter One

The lessons we learn come from all sources, and each day brings ample opportunity for our experiences to turn into growth. Sometimes we make mistakes, and other times, we get things right. We can only endure if we take an attitude of apprenticeship, meaning, we are willing to admit we do not know certain things very well and are making the best choices and decisions as we go.

So far, life had taught me that life is about a pleasant mixture of chores and play. Getting the balance right was what mattered most, and otherwise, too much of one or the other would leave one feeling despondent eventually. Also, I was beginning to understand, from listening to the conversations of the adults in my life, that humanity could be quite selfish. There seemed to be a lot of people in the world who did not care for the best interest of others. Things could get downright ugly when leaders, whether they be from business or government interests, sought only to control others instead of allowing them to pursue their own interests and lifestyle. This was a major, overriding theme in almost everything my parents, grandparents, their friends, and associates were either concerned about or bothered by the most.

By the time I turned nine, our youngest sister named Estrella had come along and my mami was pregnant with what would turn out to be our last sibling—my brother Luis. With Mami carrying the weight of another baby and busy with the baby Estrella, I assisted her as much as I could with housework and looking after Fernando and Lilliana. Still, somehow, we had some quiet moments in between, and there was an hour or two of peace and quiet in the house.

Mami had begun showing me more about how to make clothing on her old American Singer sewing machine. It was a rackety old thing, but it always surprised me in its efficiency and ability to get the work done. I marveled at how quickly the needle darted up and down and made a perfect stitch each time.

"You must keep your fingers just so as you feed the fabric," Mami told me, showing me the precise location of my left- and right-hand thumbs, indexes, and remainder of my fingers.

The first few times I tried, I was afraid I would get my fingers impaled by the needle. With patience and Mami's tireless supervision, I slowly began to overcome my fear and soon began to master the craft. *Of course, once I had learned well enough, I could make myself all sorts of new dolls!*

Besides the sewing itself, I spent time admiring Mami's other skills as a seamstress and watched fascinated as she performed all the other functions necessary in making clothing. I did not know how she did it, between the sizing, cutting, and matching patterns and designs, adding fanfare, buttons, clasps, zippers, and especially when it came time to pleat the fabric in order to put in pockets, *Mami seemed like some kind of a genius to me.*

To try helping her as much as I could, instead of her making extra trips into town, I now quite often went to the fabric supplier after school with a list Mami would compile. It was an old storefront with a large window looking in on shelves loaded with bundles, swaths, and squares of fabrics of well over hundreds of various designs. Some were one solid color, while others had many different sizes and colors of stripes or designs such as flowers, red and white plaid boxes, and bands of multiple widths.

I found there were many complications trying to get just what Mami had sought, but the owners, an older couple who had owned the store since they had married thirty years before, knew Mami's preferences well enough. They seemed to know how to select the fabric closest to what she had desired. Mr. and Mrs. Zayas were always kind and patient with me, and they encouraged that I get to know the world of fabric from a sophisticated perspective. It intrigued me that so much effort went into such things as thread count, understanding the qualities of the multitude types of fabric, learning the language which expressed each variation of shade for the primary colors, and how the cost of the fabric depended entirely upon each of these factors. Putting everything together, this gave me greater respect for Mami's work than I had ever known before, because I realized that if Mami's customers were not happy with her choice of fabric from the start, then all of the work she would put in to making the garment would be for nothing.

Now that I was nine, I had begun thinking about what kind of work I might do as I got older. Although I enjoyed sewing and helping Mami with certain, specific aspects of making dresses mostly, but also occasionally shirts, slacks, and gowns, I did not think I would like to do that for the rest of my life. After several hours at the machine, she was often tired, her hands and fingers worn, and her back ached greatly. I thought that since I loved to learn about new things, I figured perhaps I could become a teacher, or something using education, since I enjoyed school and learning so much. *Also, it would help that I was good at taking care of my younger siblings.* I had not discussed this yet with Mami or Papo since I was not entirely certain, but to me, it seemed like it might be a logical pursuit for when I became an adult.

On a cool and breezy Monday morning in October, as usual, Antonio, Josephina, Fernando, and I were walking to school early in the morning. Lilliana would start next year, and so she and Estrella were home with Mami. Our school was just outside of downtown Santa Fe on the south side of town, and since our farm was south of town, the walk usually took us only about half an hour. When it rained, sometimes Papo would drive us to school in the truck, but then he would get a late start at the yard, and so we only did this when the rain was torrential. Many children walked to school like us, while others were transported by their parents in automobiles, trucks, or horse-drawn carriages. The walk was pleasant along the quiet and calm avenue, which on our right side going to school were mostly estates and homesteads amid the pine forests, while on the left side were endless fields of crops, mostly tobacco, sugarcane, and rows of peppers, melons, coffee, and corn.

Antonio took the lead this morning as usual, and I noticed Josephina was wearing the lime green dress which I had helped Mami make a few weeks ago. It looked very pretty on her. Both Antonio and Fernando were wearing black dress shorts with short-sleeved, white button-down shirts and black shoes. I had on my rose skirt with white blouse. Each of us carried a bundle of books tied with a cord, which we held tightly in our hands over our shoulders. The trail we walked ran alongside of the avenue and was wide and well-defined. It was a beautiful morning, and I was looking forward to class. My teacher, Mrs. Allamanda, was a creative teacher who used many sorts of games and fun activities to instruct. *She was just the kind of teacher someday I would like to be should I become a teacher.*

Since I had to go to the fabric store after school, and Antonio would rush back to put a few hours in at the farm with Papa Ramon, Josephina would be walking home with Fernando today. *Sometimes, I worried that she did not have patience with him.* He was always so inquisitive and active, and I knew this got on my older sister's nerves from time to time. Breaking me out of my own inner dialogue, I suddenly heard my oldest sibling.

"How did your homework turn out, Angela," Antonio asked. He had not turned back to look at me, but nonetheless, I could hear his concern by his tone. We were about halfway to school along the main avenue, and Antonio knew I had been working diligently on an assignment for class the past three nights, a paper on Cuban history.

"Very good, I hope." I had taken out a book on history from our school library, and it was large and heavy. For over a week now, I had scoured it for information. Today, I would be reading my report to the entire class.

Suddenly, I heard Josephina's voice. "You will do fine, Angela. You always do. Me, on the other hand, I just do not know. I have a math quiz, and these percentages and fractions get on my last nerve."

Antonio looked back at Josephina while grabbing Fernando by the hand, who, while searching the ground for bugs or rocks, had unknowingly stepped out on to the avenue. "Remember what Papo always says when it comes to fractions—*think of a pie and how many slices you would need to cut the whole thing into equal shares.*"

However, Josephina was quite miffed. *"Eight slices for any pie is quite adequate!* Why will I need to know about fractions anyway? I help Papo with invoices all the time at work, and we never use them." She flapped her long hair from off her shoulder with a wave of her hand. "There's just no need for them."

None of us had an answer to appease her angst, and so we let it drop. A minute later, however, probably to break the tension now felt on behalf of my sister, Antonio said, "Anyway, I think my favorite activity today will be playing baseball during recess!"

I smiled and watched Fernando kick at a rock, sending it scuttling across the road. No cars had passed by for the last five minutes or so, but as we had gotten closer to our destination, the trail had turned into sidewalk, and more groups of children coming from side streets joined us on their way to school. We chatted with a few we knew from class or church, and about five minutes later, we finally arrived at the school's entrance. Antonio left us in order to drop-off Fernando at his class, and Josephina and I parted ways to go to our separate classrooms. Two minutes later, after walking down a long hallway with classrooms on each side, I entered mine and immediately noticed that most of my classmates were gathered around several different desks in clutters either talking or playing. There was still a few minutes before the bell would ring signaling class was in session, and so I sat at my desk. After putting my books in order and making sure I had a sharpened pencil handy, I went through my report one more time. Finding some areas that I thought would sound better with a different choice of words, I made a few changes using my eraser and pencil. I thought about the length, and although we were supposed to limit our speech to five or six minutes, I believed my report was filled with necessary information and so what if I went a few minutes longer.

Mrs. Allamanda came into the classroom just as the bell rang, and she wished us a good morning and welcomed us to another fun-filled day of learning. All through our Spanish, civics, and math lessons, I became increasingly anxious as I imagined myself before my classmates, speaking as if I was a scholar on the subject of Cuban history. I tried occasionally glancing back at my classmates to see if anyone else seemed to be on edge, but I could not be sure. Finally, just before lunch, it was time for our history lesson.

"I had assigned four students to give their report before the class today, and so let's get right to them," Mrs. Allamanda said.

My heart skipped a beat as I figured I would be called first. I tried looking away, out the window where some of the older boys were in the yard playing baseball. As I was searching to see if I could find my brother, I felt my teacher staring at me. I turned back to look at her, and I immediately knew I had been correct.

"Angela, won't you be a dear and go first?" Mrs. Allamanda asked me.

Although I briefly considered responding by saying that I wished to go third or fourth, I did not honestly believe that I had a choice in the matter. So instead, I nodded and stood up, and taking my four-page handwritten report from my desk, I walked to the front of the classroom. Mrs. Allamanda was smiling as I approached, but when I turned to face my classmates, I noticed expressions ranging from boredom and undue interest, to downright scorn and hostility. Bracing myself, I thought, *it was now or never!*

My voice was too quiet right at first, but then due to coaching from the sidelines, meaning Mrs. Allamanda pointing her thumb straight up into the air, I found a volume and tone that seemed to suit the situation.

"The Spanish explorer Christopher Columbus first sighted the northern coast of Cuba on October 27, 1492. He was able to make landfall on our island the following day." I looked out at my classmates and was surprised to see that they all seemed to be listening and not sleeping or playing. "Historians believe the name *Cuba* comes from a language known as the Taíno language, and its word *cubao*, which, when translated from Taíno, means *where fertile land is abundant*. Native islanders from many islands around the Gulf of Mexico had used the Taíno language until it became extinct in the sixteenth century." I paused and took a deep breath. "By the year 1511, Spanish conquistador Diego Velázquez de Cuéllar began to settle the island of Cuba with permanent residents by bringing mostly Spanish citizens, along with their African slaves. Domestic planners back in Spain divided Cuba into seven divisions, including Havana, Santiago, and Santo Domingo."

I looked to my right at Mrs. Allamanda, and she seemed pleased. "Each municipality had its own *cabildo*, or town council, which governed its business affairs. Elected representatives of each *cabildo* formed a governing body before the royal council, where they negotiated economic matters. Conquistadors were granted control over the Indians in specific areas and were given the right to demand goods from them. This was a sad time though since the Indian population had decreased greatly due to diseases from Europe. By 1570, many new generations of Cubans were comprised between Spanish, African, and Indian heritages, making colonial society very diverse since both its Spanish-born and American-born citizens shared their customs and traditions." I flipped over the first page. "During the eighteenth century, Cuba depended upon the sugarcane crop and relied upon plantations where the workers were mainly slaves. In 1740, the Havana Company was formed, and its purpose was to stimulate agriculture across the island."

I looked up at the large clock above the door to the classroom and realized I had already spoken for four minutes and had not even gotten to the important information. I started panicking a bit and reading faster. "By 1860, the island's population had increased from one hundred fifty thousand to almost a million and a half. Families were large, and almost everybody joined in to work and share the burdens of farm life. Only women of the upper classes did not work, and many of them were able to attain higher levels of education. For most people, life was difficult, even in the largest of Cuban cities. The demands of producing sugar required so many laborers, money, machines, and technical skills. The economic differences between Spanish-run cities and colonists who owned the farms was tremendous, and soon the farmers realized that Spanish rule was corrupt, unfair, and too strict." I looked up, and my classmates were following with interest. *I could not believe it!* "In 1868, Spain started the first war for Cuban independence, which was called the Ten Years' War, because they kept on increasing taxes on the farmers and refusing to grant Cubans a say in how they were governed."

This next part I had added just last night, and though important, now I feared that it really put me over my allotment of time.

"It had been on October 10, 1868, that the eastern farmer Carlos Manuel de Céspedes issued the Grito de Yara decree, in which he declared Cuban independence. He freed his slaves to fight in his revolution and encouraged other farmers to do the same. By then, even many people in the United States announced their anger at Spain's treatment of its colonists. He had been a humble man who had been pushed too far. After receiving his baccalaureate degree from Havana University in 1840, Céspedes then completed his law studies in Spain. Upon his return to Cuba, he started a law practice, wrote poems and pamphlets, and secretly organized an independence movement. In 1868, he was made chief of the revolutionary movement in the Oriente region, and the revolution gained momentum. Soon, over twelve thousand volunteers had joined, and they were beating the Spanish troops. However, Spanish troops began to pour into Cuba, and the earlier victories were followed by defeats and retreats for the freedom fighters."

Mrs. Allamanda was spinning her index fingers around in circles, indicating for me to speed it up. I was now on page three and had this page and one more to go. "Céspedes was elected president by the revolutionary government, and the first thing he did was to free the slaves and write a new constitution. Once Spain began to overpower Cuban forces, Céspedes was forced into hiding and then discovered and shot by Spanish soldiers. Although his revolution eventually failed, Céspedes is credited with beginning the movement which would finally lead to Cuban independence almost twenty years later. He is known as the father of our country. In 1910, his remains were placed in the National Pantheon of Heroes of the Cuban Revolution in Havana."

I lost my place momentarily and had to scroll down the page with my finger until I found where I had left off. "Black Cubans became the backbone of the Cuban independence movement after this war, and its Liberation Army were called Los Mambises. One of their soldiers, Antonio Maceo, was one of the greatest military commanders in both the Ten Years' War and the next war for independence to come, in 1895. He was often called the Bronze Titan, and he was one of the most important leaders in Cuba's fight for independence. Spain promised to assist Cubans and their economic welfare in the Pact of Zanjón of 1878, which ended the first war. However, Antonio Maceo and several other generals refused to accept the Spanish conditions, and quickly, the political and economic tensions grew once again. The Spanish government failed to carry out most of the promised reforms, and they began policies which hurt the farmers worse than before. Then Spain created more taxes and stopped allowing the farmers to sell their goods to other countries. That is when the Cuban poet, José Martí, put together another plan for independence. He had gotten support from the United States, and the Second War for Independence broke out on February 24, 1895. Martí and his friend, General Máximo Gómez, planned to work together to beat the Spanish once and for all."

I had grown tired myself speaking too fast, and I stopped. Mrs. Allamanda looked at me with a questioning stare. I still had a page and a half to go, and I did not know if I should proceed. Ten minutes had now flown by and I looked at my classmates and they seemed to be wondering why I had stopped.

Mrs. Allamanda then took a few steps closer to me and toward the center of the classroom. She then said, "Class, it seems Angela has truly done a very thorough and comprehensive report. Really, it is beyond my expectations and is something a student four years her senior might be expected to produce. Angela, do you have much more to go?"

I did not know what to say. It was the first time I realized that I understood my country more extensively than most of my peers. Listening to Papo and Papa Ramon and their friends all these years had culled within me an appreciation for politics and government. I had believed up until then that I was just doing what had been expected as far as the assignment. A bit embarrassed, I looked the final page of my report and responded, "Just a bit more. I can go quickly."

"No, Angela, that is okay. It seems everybody is enjoying your thoroughness. Please finish as you were doing. We can move one of the other students to give their presentation tomorrow." She smiled and took a few steps back to where she had been standing.

I cleared my throat, smiled in return, and then continued. "The battles of this second war were fierce and soon spread throughout our island. Spain continued sending many troops to Cuba to defeat the Liberation Army. Finally, one day, they followed the Cuban hero, the Bronze Titan Antonio Maceo, and they had a sneak attack, killing him and General Máximo Gómez's son, Panchito Gómez Toro, who had become close partners in battle. Many believed the war would be over now since Cuba had lost two of its greatest heroes, Maceo and Céspedes. However, another hero stepped up. A farmer by the name of Juan Delgado, who had just recently joined the ranks of the freedom fighters. With courage beyond most men, he took fighters on horseback, and with his machete raised high, he charged into the woods, full of Spanish troops, in order to recover the bodies of Maceo and Toro. He knew that if Spain had recovered the bodies, they would have shown the Cubans that their hero was dead by bringing the bodies through all of the cities and villages of Cuba.

"Colonel Juan Delgado and his men found the bodies amidst constant enemy gunfire, and they recovered them. Riding by horseback all night, they brought the bodies to Juan Delgado's uncle, Pedro Perez, and to his farm on the Cacahual in Bejucal. There and then, they swore a pact of secrecy as they buried the bodies far away from the homestead upon the mountain. Spanish soldiers were sent door-to-door in search of the bodies, but Pedro Perez had sworn to his nephew and his oldest sons the famous *Pact of Silence*, meaning they would never tell any enemy about having the bodies in their possession. Spanish soldiers did not believe Pedro when they asked if he knew where the bodies had been buried. They then tortured Pedro Perez's oldest son, Romualdo, in front of his entire family and even when he died from the torture days later, still nobody said a word. That is why Juan Delgado and Pedro Perez and his family are honored by statues and plaques throughout Cuba today. Their mission has been credited with Cuba's independence ever since."

I looked and it seemed my classmates were captivated by these truths. I felt a sudden jolt of euphoria, or something close to it, that my words had such an impact. "When Spain's Navy blew up the US battleship, the USS *Maine*, in Havana Harbor a year later, on

February 15, 1898, the US declared war on Spain. By this time, Spain was weakened by all the fighting they had endured, and they soon surrendered. Cuban independence was granted by the Treaty of Paris on December 10, 1898, but US forces continued to occupy Cuba. At first, the United States tried to exclude Cubans from the new government. But soon, the role of Cubans in government increased with supervised elections, and Cuba then elected its first president, Tomás Estrada Palma. US military forces did help to modernize Havana by expanding its harbor and building new schools, roads, and bridges. But they were really interested in importing US influence to the island. The United States gave themselves the right to oversee Cuba's international commitments, economy, and internal affairs and to establish a naval station at Guantánamo Bay on the island's southeastern coast."

I knew I was almost finished, and this last part, though not as entertaining perhaps, was every bit as important. I emphasized each part of it so that my classmates might understand the situation we currently endured as a nation. "Estrada Palma tried to retain power in the next elections in 1905, but there was another rebellion. Estrada Palma finally resigned, and the US government then made Charles Magoon provisional president. In January 1909, Magoon handed over the government to José Miguel Gómez. Even though Cuba's economy grew steadily, the Gómez administration was corrupt and full of many bad policies which wasted Cuba's money. Much corruption continued under the next several administrations of Mario García Menocal, who was president until 1921, then Alfredo Zayas until 1925, and finally Gerardo Machado y Morales. *Machado was known as one of the worst presidents because he used manipulation, his military, and even assassinations to get what he wanted.* All these leaders were interested in their own wealth at the expense of us citizens. The US government helped our government to overthrow him last year in the Revolution of 1933, which really was only a small skirmish in Havana, but it brought our newest president, Fulgencio Batista, to power. Now that we have Fulgencio Batista, we hope we will be a free and upright government and country, a democracy finally full of healthy and joyful citizens."

I stopped and looked up. When they realized I had finished, everyone stood up and began to clap. I believe I had even seen a tear or two in Mrs. Allamanda's eyes.

My Mami's sister Lucia lived five blocks from our house in the northeastern most point of Santa Fe. She and her husband, Juan, owned a small café there, and they had two daughters—Maria Del Carmen, my brother Antonio's age and who we simply called *Maria*, and Carmen, who was my age. At that point in time, I loved my aunt and uncle, and even possibly Maria, but I must admit, I had a difficult time with Carmen. She was insistent on always competing with me in all things, and she liked to always prove that she was smarter, tougher, and better than me in as many ways as she could. *To me, she was just sassier, and that was it.* She would come to our house to stay after school two or three days per week until her parents would close the café and come pick her up later in the evening.

One day, we were in my bedroom, which I now shared with both Josephina and Lilliana, playing with all my dolls. Carmen was about my height, with short and curly black hair and a broad face. She could be very pretty if she wanted to be, but mostly, she seemed content to have a rugged demeanor. As I set up a party for the family, celebrating Isabel's ninth birthday, it seemed to me that Carmen felt like she was above any of this foolish *little girl* play. Even so, over the most recent past several months, I had noticed that Carmen had quite a unique fascination with my dolls. *Even though she did not want to play with them*, she was always fixing their hair, straightening their clothes, or trying to test the flexibility and durability of their appendages. As I finished setting up the cups, plates, and silverware for Isabel's party, I turned to arrange the dolls and suddenly saw that Isabel was not there with the rest.

"Where's Isabel?" I asked Carmen at once.

In a voice full of feigned sympathy, Carmen responded, "She said she was not feeling well and wanted to lie down."

In her eyes, I saw a mischievous intent. With firmness in my expression, I asked, "So, where is she lying down?"

Carmen stared at me for a moment without a ripple of concern, but with a staunch tenacity instead. "She wanted fresh air, and so I put her on the window ledge."

I looked at my window and realized it was wide open and the sheers had been moved. I walked to the window and looked down on to the ground. My poor little Isabel was lying face down in the dirt. I was so angry, but I did not want Carmen to win and so would not show my emotions. Instead, I called right away to Fernando, who was sitting at the desk at the other end of the room, drawing on paper with colored pencils. "Fernando, please—you must run outside right away and get Isabel from off the ground and bring her here or she will be late for her party."

Fernando looked up from his drawing. "Why is she outside by herself on the ground?"

Covering for Carmen, I said, "She accidently fell from the window while she was looking outside." All this time, Carmen kept her vision focused on me to see if I would show any signs of weakness. I played it as cool as can be, as if everything happening was all quite natural and common. Fernando shrugged his shoulders, got up from his chair, and sauntered out the bedroom door. I began arranging the Mami and Papo, Marissa, and each of the guests who had come to the party. Carmen had gone to Fernando's drawings meantime and seemed to be wondering what mischief she could do there. I kept a close eye on her as a moment later, Fernando returned with Isabel, who had a bit of dirt on her face. As I wiped this off with the bottom of my shirt, Carmen came to the dolls and began pouring water for them, as if nothing had happened.

As we played, I could tell Carmen would rather be anywhere else but inside the bedroom. She was not at all helping me, and finally, having enough of her distant involvement, I said, "Party's over." I began putting all the puppets and everything else we were using away in their places.

"Let's go outside and play in the yard," Carmen said. "We can catch bugs and keep them in jars."

Even though it was precisely the last thing in the world I wanted to do, in order to keep peace between us, I made believe it was a marvelous idea and said, "Okay."

We played outside for almost an hour and then had a quiet dinner. I knew Mami could tell there was a bit of tension between Carmen and I, but she did not mention it. Papo had a long day and seemed very tired, and it was mostly Antonio who talked during the meal, bragging almost incessantly about how well his baseball team was doing. After cleaning up, *and might I mention with very little assistance from Carmen,* who had disappeared two or three times while Josephina, Mami, and I did all the work, thankfully, Aunt Lucia came with Maria to retrieve Carmen for the night. I was a bit upset that Mami had reported to Aunt Lucia that Carmen had been very well-behaved and was no problem at all. *No problem for her, perhaps.*

Then something happened which would forever change the nature of my relationship with Carmen once and for all. When I went to my room to get ready for bed later that evening, *I immediately noticed Isabel was missing.* I had remembered putting her back where I always do, right next to Marissa on the top of my bureau. *I knew right away that Carmen had kidnapped Isabel.* Although I was upset, I did not want to bother Mami or Papo as they were both extremely tired from all their efforts throughout the day. The next day, I saw Carmen out in the playground during recess.

"Please bring Isabel home to me. You can bring her to school tomorrow or to my house after school."

She gave me a stern look. Her face took an ugly demeanor, and I remember at that moment that I wanted to punch it. "What do you mean? I don't have Isabel. Are you sure she didn't fall from the window again while looking outside? She is probably lying in the dirt again just outside of your window."

Inside, I felt so furious and do not believe up until that time I had ever known such fury. It was seeing the face of cruelty itself for no other reason but to upset another that hit me like a lead weight right in the gut. Before tears came to my eyes, I turned and walked back to my classroom. I calmed myself as best I could to get through the afternoon. The next day, Carmen avoided me at school, and I did not walk with her to my house after school. I got home first, and when she had arrived, I went to my bedroom and closed the door. Mami left me alone, and I cannot say I knew what Carmen did while I brooded on my bed. At dinner, I was silent.

Two more days of this and I had enough. On Saturday morning, after breakfast, I knew Carmen would be with her parents at the café most of the day. I told Mami I was going outside to play in the backyard, but instead I marched through the small area of woods behind our yard and out on to the main avenue. I took a quick right at the first side road and kept on walking. It was a bit strange as I had not walked by myself down this road before that. I felt like those passing me by and living in the homes along the road were wondering what a young girl was doing walking by herself. *It did not matter—I had a mission.*

About ten minutes later, I arrived at Aunt Lucia and Uncle Juan's house. As I had hoped, when I went to the side of the house, knowing where Carmen's bedroom was, the window was open. I lifted it a bit higher, and then hoisted myself up with my hands on to the window ledge. Carefully, I crawled through the opening and jumped down on to her bedroom floor a moment later. Her room was a mess—things thrown everywhere, dirty clothes, old toys, and her bed was unmade. Immediately, I felt both disgusted and sorry for anyone who chose to live this way. I knew it was very likely that Carmen would not have left Isabel out in the open, just in case her Mami came looking in her room and recognized my doll. I immediately went to her closet and bent down to push aside a pile of clothes on the floor. There, bringing me an immediate pang of relief and joy, Isabel was lying on her back with the same comforting smile that she always had. I picked her up and held her close to my chest for quite some time. I checked her closely and she seemed to be unharmed. Instead of going out the window, I walked through the house and let myself out the front door. I do not remember having locked the door when I closed it behind me, but at that point, *I did not care.*

Mami checked on me almost immediately after I had returned. I was in my usual play area in the backyard with Isabel on my lap as we sat in the swing chair. Mami asked, "Sweetie, are you okay this morning?"

I smiled and held up Isabel. "I had lost Isabel, but now I got her back!"

Mami gave me a perplexed look, but then she smiled as if she had suddenly understood. "I will go and get you both something to drink."

As she was walking back toward the house, I said, "Carmen needs us to teach her some better manners, Mami."

Glancing back at me over her shoulder, she said, "Isn't that the truth!"

On Monday, after school, Carmen arrived at our house about ten minutes after me. I had been working on a new doll by myself for about two weeks. She looked good to me—with red hair and rosy cheeks, a button-down blue sweater, and a cream-colored skirt, I knew she was my prettiest doll yet. I believed Carmen would go out to the swing chair when she got to my house since she and I were still not talking, and I had prepared by putting my new doll, Sadie, out on it. I listened as she came into the kitchen and talked with Mami for a while. As I expected, after about ten minutes, she said she was going out to play. *To this day, I am thankful to Mami that she never tried to get involved in my affairs with friends or siblings, unless I asked for her help.* I waited about five minutes and then I strolled out into the backyard.

What I found changed my view of Carmen for good. Carmen had Sadie on her lap and was humming to her while brushing her hair. Quite surprised when she looked up to see me walking out toward them, she abruptly stopped humming and pushed Sadie away. I sat beside her on the chair and picked up Sadie.

"You don't have to make believe you don't like playing with dolls, Carmen." I turned to look at her, and she just shrugged. "Besides, I made Sadie just for you. What will she think if her new mami does not want to hold her in her lap and hum to her once in a while?" I held Sadie out to Carmen.

I suppose it was my invitation for her to enjoy her role as caretaker that might have made the difference. Carmen suddenly smiled despite herself, and then suddenly began laughing. She took Sadie into her arms and hugged her close to her chest. We had a party for

Sadie that afternoon, and Carmen was thoroughly involved. From that day on, Carmen and I became best friends.

On a Monday morning a few weeks later, on a day when there was no school due to teacher meetings, I went with Papo and my two older siblings to the lumberyard in order to offer my assistance. Mostly, I stayed with Josephina, watching her do the tasks which Papo had assigned to her. There were four small connected offices, each having walls of large windows giving view into each of the other offices, and which together made up the administrative heart of my papo's business. These were located just off the main factory, and Papo had two regular office staff. One was a receptionist named Wanda, and the other, the bookkeeper named Miguel. Wanda was very energetic and friendly, whereas Miguel dressed very formally and was quiet in a reserved way, not a mean one. Josephina and I started off by sweeping the offices, emptying the trash bins, and straightening out in general.

An hour into it, I got my wish. Papo came in from the yard and asked that Josephina and I follow him and Antonio. For the first time, I would be witnessing the entire lumberyard in action on a busy workday. First of all, I soon realized just how many men Papo had working for him. It seemed to be more than thirty altogether, but I lost count after about twenty or so. There were so many large table saws constantly buzzing in almost every area of the yard, and these made a constant and ear-piercing high-pitched squeal. Two or three men worked each of the large table saws, while others used handheld saws by themselves. Some of the workers had on goggles, and others wore clear plastic shields over their entire faces. All had on thick leather gloves which made their hands appear two times the normal size. We made a sweep of all the outdoor work areas, and I was amazed at how large and how many piles of lumber extended all around the perimeter of the yard. I loved the smell of the fresh pine dust, and it became somewhat intoxicating after a while. Many workers were sorting the lumber as they busily chatted to each other about this and that, but several seemed to know Antonio quite well, and they waved and said hello with a smile as we passed.

Occasionally, Antonio and Papo would stop to help some of the men putting several of the finished beams on the highest part of a pile. Sometimes Papo would stop and offer his advice about a length or cutting angle. I must admit that I felt like a bigwig strolling along with my brother and sister, and of course, *the man who all these men called boss*. I felt proud of Papo, but more importantly, for my entire family, for the achievement of having such a successful business that gave so many workers a means to care for their families. When we finished the tour, my sister and I went to the smallest of the offices, behind the two larger outer offices. We sat at a desk, and Josephina then explained to me why it was important to file each of the invoices, letters, statements, and bills, which were in various piles before us, into their appropriate folders. There were four large filing cabinets behind us against the far back wall, and she showed me that the folders inside them were alphabetically sorted by company name. In the case where the customer or supplier was an individual and not a company, then by last name first.

I started working, and Josephina kept close watch on my filing ability. Occasionally, she would stop me, saying we have to do it this way or that because that is how Miguel wanted things done. Mostly, it had to do with what to staple, what to paper clip, and which page should appear on top. About an hour into this, I looked up from the desk and coming into the outside office were Papo's sister Beatriz Martinez, her husband, Pablito, and their daughter, my cousin Caruca. I was surprised to see them here, and Josephina stopped me from getting up right away.

"Finish those two invoices first," she said, pointing at two pages I had put to the side of my work pile.

My Aunt Beatriz and her family lived in a beautiful home in downtown Santa Fe, close to our church. They owned a general store further north of town, which was always quite busy. Their store sold everything from food to pharmaceutics, clothing, shoes, and jewelry, to fresh baked cookies. Caruca was Antonio's age and helped at the store quite often. She was tall with an elegant yet narrow face, had long brown hair, and I remember I always saw her in woman's business attire. The entire family remained so busy at the store that we did not get together that often with them. However, when we did, we would always have a great time. My aunt and uncle were quite jovial when they were together, and they let us know that they loved us very much.

Josephina and I finished for now and met them out in the larger front office. Upon seeing us, they gave us hugs. Soon Papo and Antonio came in. As Caruca talked about all the things going on at the store, I realized I admired her knowledge and her assertations about how much she would accomplish in all of her various roles there. Uncle Pablito finally informed that they were here to get some lumber as they were having their workers build a storage shed out back, behind the general store. Papo picked out the best planks for them and had his men load it on to Uncle Pablito's truck. He said proudly, "No charge," when Uncle asked him how much for the wood. Uncle and Aunt then promised to invite us to an outdoor meal in their backyard once the shed was finished.

It bears mentioning both Mami and Papo had relatives as far away as Havana, and we usually only heard from them one or two times per year. As Christmas approached, I always thought of our relatives and how they would be celebrating the birth of Jesus, especially since many cities back on the mainland island of Cuba had marvelous celebrations during the week from Christmas through New Year's Day. Although we did not like to be away from home too often, and the holidays were magnificent right here in Santa Fe, we had heard so much about the holiday festivities on the mainland, and particularly about the Charanga celebration in Bejucal, about an hour south of Havana by auto. A huge parade with all kinds of floats and people from all classes coming together dancing and singing throughout the streets all night long—*what a spectacle it must be!* Hearing about such fun made me want to go there to participate in it. *One day, I would make it there, or perhaps even to Havana!*

Chapter Two

By the middle of November, with the harvest in and mostly all distributed, we finally had time to catch our breath and slow down a bit. Papa Ramon still had one large storage barn full of crop, and Pilar and I loved walking through it to see a portion of all the food the farm had produced that year. We would feel and smell the freshness of the pumpkins, corn, peppers, and melons to check and make sure they were still good. Once in a while, I would pop a fresh, sweet pepper in my mouth and crunch on it. I would dare to taste one of the varieties of the hot peppers as well, but just a bit of it. We would then make our way to the barn where the horses lived and give them some hay, touch their noses if they would let us, and talk to some of them. Pilar's favorite was a rust-colored Arabian named Simon, whose coat was shiny and smooth and who seemed to smile at her the entire time we visited. I loved the pony Vick, who was small and yet dignified in his mannerisms and affections.

One Saturday, after visiting our horses, we went to the cow pens attached to the next barn. We watched them grazing on the grass until one large heifer, who was all brown except for three white legs, came sauntering over to us. Her huge eyes were fixed on us as she neared the wooden fence. Suddenly, she opened her mouth and let out a loud and extended *moo*. Pilar looked at me and started to laugh. "I think she's saying hello," she said.

To me, it seemed more like the heifer was protesting. I carefully began to extend my arm out toward her. She watched my approaching hand very carefully, and I saw concern in her eyes, but then suddenly, she lifted her mouth and rubbed her nose against my forearm. It felt warm and moist, and the next thing I knew, her lips were surrounding my fingers, and I felt her nibbling gently on them. Pilar was astonished and seemed to be holding her breath. I realized that the young cow had hoped I had some treats in my hand to offer. I gently massaged her upper lips as she stuck her tongue into my palm. I patted her nose and said, "Sorry, girl. I have nothing for you. We'll come back soon, and I'll have something!"

We started back toward the storage barn. This year, Papa Ramon had decided to try growing several rows of carrots, and they had turned out better than he had expected. We entered the barn and, about midway through, found the carrots. I grabbed two medium-sized from the wooden crate for Pilar and two for me, and we walked back to the pen. Sure enough, the heifer, who from that day on I named *Lovey*, was waiting by the fence as if she had fully understood my words to her and had trusted I would be doing as I had said by returning with treats. Realizing that Papa Ramon and Abuela had more animals on their farm than did Pilar's parents, who only had pigs and chickens on theirs, I knew Pilar did not have much experience with large animals, and I was intent on helping her to learn how to care for them.

I let her know she could go and give Lovey the carrots; however, she was hesitant extending her arm out or getting too close. As Lovey's big brown eyes stared intently at Pilar's face, I said, "Go ahead, it's okay." Pilar took another step closer, but she was still two steps away from reaching the cow even with her arm outstretched. As her hand waved the carrot out toward Lovey's mouth, suddenly, impatient, Lovey mooed quite loudly. Pilar reacted by backing up two steps. "Pilar!" I protested. Changing my strategy, I walked to the fence and put a carrot right before Lovey's mouth. She quickly and eagerly took it out of my palm with her mouth with no problems. "See!" I said. "It's easy. She won't hurt you." I backed up two steps and put my hand on Pilar's shoulder, nudging her forward. "Now, it's your turn."

"You sure she won't bite my fingers?" Pilar asked, looking up at me with a bit of fear in her expression.

"I promise she won't. They know to be gentle when getting something from people." I looked at Lovey, who seemed to understand that coaxing the carrot from my best friend was not going to work. She, too, changed strategies and put her head down into the grass and began munching on some tall strands coming up from around one of the fence poles. "See, she's letting you know she can wait until you're ready."

Pilar took a slow but steady step forward. Her eyes remained glued on Lovey, who was acting like she could not care less about the carrot now. Glancing at me for reassurance, Pilar was ready to take the next step, and I nodded at her to do so. Having gained a bit of confidence, most likely due to Lovey's ingenious plan to not look at my friend, Pilar took another step and then one more. She was now in position, and she stuck her right hand with one of the carrots between the openings of the wooden panels of the fence. By now, Lovey had displayed all the temperate attitude that she could stand. Her mouth came straight up at Pilar, her eyes larger than ever, and her lips took the carrot from my best friend's hand before Pilar could even think to react. Even with such haste to get the carrot before Pilar could change her mind or back up out of fear, I think it amazed Pilar how gentle Lovey was when she took the carrot from her.

Without my prompting, Pilar took the second carrot out from the pocket of her dress, and this time without hesitation, she gave it to Lovey. She even left her hand there until after Lovey had finished chewing and swallowing the carrot.

"It tickles," Pilar said, suddenly giggling, as Lovey licked her palm with a rather large and pink tongue.

I gave her my second carrot to give to Lovey, and after that, they had become best friends.

On the way back to the house, we saw Papa Ramon entering the storage barn. Right behind him was a tall man dressed in a fancy business suit, and as I looked more closely, I could see it was Mr. Smith, the American buyer. We picked up our pace, and I waved my hand at them, calling out, "Papa Ramon, wait for us!" Mr. Smith heard us first, and he turned to see us, and then Papa Ramon backed out of the barn, looking at us coming toward them from around the corner of the barn door. "C'mon," I said to Pilar as I started running toward the two men, Pilar keeping up just a few steps behind me.

Papa Ramon and Mr. Smith waited by the door to the storage barn until we arrived.

"Well, look who we have here!" Mr. Smith said in his best broken Spanish, which was not too bad, although he would get the pronouns wrong occasionally. His voice was light and airy. He was a jovial man, probably in his forties, plump, with a round face complimented by two rosy cheeks. The thinning light-brown hair on top of his head came across his forehead in a few lonely strands.

I smiled and looked up at him expectantly. "Hello, Mr. Smith, how are you today?"

"Wonderful, darling. Just wonderful," Mr. Smith responded and then reached into the pocket of his business coat.

Papa Ramon shook his head. "You spoil my granddaughter."

"And who is your friend?" the American asked me, ignoring Papa. He then took something from his jacket pocket but kept it close to his chest so we could not see what it was.

I lifted my hand in Pilar's direction. "This is my best friend in the whole world, Pilar!"

"Well, ladies, today is your lucky day." With his free hand, he unwrapped tissue paper from whatever it was he was holding in his other hand. "I have something for you right from the best toy shop in all of New York City, possibly the entire United States." He brought his hand down to us and opened it. Within his palm were three lovely little glistening, ceramic dresser-doll figurines, each the size of my pinkie finger. I quickly looked them over and then took one of them out of his hand to examine it more closely. She had a smiling face with deep blue eyes, auburn brown hair, pink lips, and rosy cheeks just like Mr. Smith himself. She wore a beautiful pearl white dress which had a corsage of purple flowers attached to the shoulder strap. Some of the same flowers were in her hair attached to a tie which kept her hair parted neatly to her right side. Her neckline was stunningly smooth and clear, as were her elegant arms, which rested easily at her sides. I looked back at the other two figurines in his hand and realized that each of them were similar, but with very minor variations. I knew right away that mine was the prettiest because her face was just picture perfect!

Finally satisfied, I held her up to Papa Ramon. "Look, Papa Ramon, she is beautiful!"

"Go ahead and give one to your friend," Mr. Smith said, smiling and content that he had found a gift worthy of my tastes.

I turned to Pillar and nodded at her. She approached Mr. Smith's open hand and tentatively looked at both remaining figurines, pushing them over with her finger to examine each more closely. As she was deciding, I asked Mr. Smith, "Who is the third one for?"

He cleared his throat. "Well, to tell the truth, I have one more stop to make this afternoon and had a special little girl in mind there." I nodded in reply.

Pilar finally chose one of the ladies and had selected the one I would have picked as my second choice, even though I knew that I had taken the prettiest one. She held it up to my eyes for me to examine. "She is gorgeous, Pilar." I turned and smiled at Mr. Smith. "Thank you, Mr. Smith!"

"Yes, thank you, Mr. Smith," Pilar echoed. She turned to me, and we had our dress-doll figurines engage one another, smiling and having them say hello, and even kissing one another in friendship. I then put mine safely in my dress pocket, and Pilar did the same.

Papa Ramon led the way into the storage barn, and we followed them. Mr. Smith began looking over all the rows and stacks of produce. As we walked down the center aisle of the barn, they were talking casually to one another. I did not hear much of what they were discussing until I heard Papo Ramon asking Mr. Smith, "Were you actually all the way north into New York City to buy those figurines?"

I was listening closely now since I was curious about his answer. I knew Mr. Smith lived along the coast of the state they called Louisiana and that New York would have been a far trip for him to have taken just to get figurines.

Somewhat absently, as he looked up and down the rows of boxes of assorted peppers, Mr. Smith responded, "Yes, Ramon, the missus had been nagging me about a trip to New York for the past six months. In America, we must *try to always* keep our women happy. Otherwise, hell awaits us men!" He paused, and I could not tell if he was serious or joking. He turned back to look at Papo Ramon, then he smiled and winked at him as he said, "When they want something, you have to listen. I am sure you must know what I mean."

Papa Ramon laughed. "Well, here in Cuba, we just assume the women in our lives are in charge, and we accept that." His face took a sudden serious turn. "However, here *in our beloved country,* women do not demand so much, and they hope to contribute to their families as much as they can. In fact, *they expect* that they will have to work hard to get the things they will need for themselves and their loved ones. Perhaps that is what is so different between your women and ours."

Mr. Smith felt some of the melons, and then went to the corn. "*And what a big difference that is,* my friend. In our country, we seem to never be able to do enough to keep our women happy no matter how much we work! They always want more, more...*more!*" Now he had grown serious, and as he thought about it, he was not finished with his plea. "I guess you could say that our women expect shiny things and elegant things and *all the newest things.* Drives a man crazy." He turned and looked back at Papa Ramon. "I think it is America itself that makes them feel like they constantly need more things in order to be happy. And we have so much to choose from—*way too much if you ask me!*"

Papa Ramon nodded. "Yes, I can see how that would be a problem." There was a pause and then Papa continued. "Hopefully, *it does not turn out* that the rest of the world's women think they must have everything your women have!"

"Oh, don't worry, Ramon, they will. *It's stupid human nature.*" Mr. Smith walked a few steps toward the center of the aisle and looked over the remaining stacks of fresh fruit and vegetables on each side of the barn. "Last month, I took all of your pumpkins, and that turned out very well for me. Everything here looks so great, and I am going to take all of it—even the carrots!"

My heart skipped a beat when I heard him say he would take the carrots, and Pilar glanced at me expressing the same thought I was having. I would not disappoint Lovey, and so I quickly interjected with an objection, asking Papa Ramon if I could keep a box or two of carrots for her. He understood my desire, nodded at me, and then looked at Mr. Smith, who expressed his consent that we may keep two boxes of the carrots. I was happy at first, but then the American said something that would quickly irk me to no end. "They learn early, Ramon. *Very early!"* He laughed, and at that moment, I was not sure what he had meant. I smiled anyway, and he and Papa agreed upon a price for the remainder of the yield. "I will have the men come around four o'clock this afternoon to pick up everything," Mr. Smith said. We walked out of the barn, and Mr. Smith turned to us and said, "Girls, enjoy your new toys. Have a wonderful Christmas, and I will see you in the springtime!"

Even though he was smiling and pleasant, I now had a different view of him than I had previously. Nonetheless, we smiled and thanked him again; however, later that evening, when Papa Ramon went out to make one more round of the lower fields on the tractor, I planned on talking this over with Abuela. After we cleaned up from dinner, I showed Abuela my beautiful new statuette, and then told her about the conversation between grandfather and Mr. Smith. She listened intently to the entire discourse, nodding every now and then.

When I had finished, I could see right away that Abuela understood my feelings of betrayal by someone I had liked. She looked at me with deeply compassionate eyes and said, "Men will complain about women, and women will complain about men, Angela. It's natural, and no harm is meant by it." Abuela got up from her chair and retrieved a cup from the counter, and then sat down beside me once again. "They love each other, and so they learn to put up with little bothersome things done by the other which are inconvenient."

As I admired my tiny ceramic lady, I replied, "It bothered me when he said *they learn early*. Maybe I should not take anything else from him if he thinks that all I care about is getting stupid things from him."

"Do not be upset or angry, my sweetheart. He meant nothing by it. Let him give you what he wants. It probably makes him feel good doing so, and if he chooses to give you things with no other motive in mind, then no harm can come from taking them."

I put the figurine aside at the center of the table. "Yes, but I work hard and contribute to doing chores and doing little things *for everyone*. Why would he say such a thing about me?"

Abuela sipped from the cold cup of coffee she had made for herself long before dinner. "Perhaps he is confused because in America, the women make the men feel they have to always give things to them to prove their love. I would say that probably his own daughters ask too much from him, maybe even his wife, and he thinks he has to buy their love. Those Americans can be good people, but sometimes they are shallow and *put too much emphasis on things that do not matter.* I think we Cubans have stronger values than that, and whether you are a man or a woman, we *all know we must help each other* to get things done. Women here really don't expect much in return except for a man to provide what he can and not more than that."

I would remember many of Abuela's lessons for the rest of my life, but I think it would be this lesson more than the rest that was of most importance to me.

By the middle of December, we were all happily anticipating Christmas. At the end of November, Mami had given birth to our youngest brother, Luis, who was cute and dimply and who already had quite a robust personality. Now three weeks old, he smiled almost every time one of us held him, tickled him, or poked our faces into his. Sometimes it seemed he tried to copy our facial expressions and even make sounds which mimicked our voices, and other times, he would stick his tongue out at us in a hilarious fashion. *He was a joy and brought us all a great deal of laughter.*

We would be having our grand Christmas celebration, as usual, at Abuela and Papo Ramon's house on Christmas Eve, with all our nearby relatives planning on coming along. As always, Abuela would be making everybody's favorite Cuban deserts, and I would be helping her, *along with making four batches of tortas with Papa Ramon!* In anticipation of getting everything we would need during the week of preparation, on the Friday before the big day the following Thursday,

Papa Ramon and I took a walk into town to get supplies. I started off skipping down the trail beside the main avenue, but I was going too fast for Papa Ramon, and so I slowed down to a brisk walk so he could keep up with me. "We need more sugar, bananas, lemons, rice, vanilla beans, and of course, more flour!" I insisted.

"Yes, my pumpkin, we shall get all of those and more," Papa Ramon replied. "Don't forget about the almonds!"

As I thought about everything we would be buying, I said, "We should have taken the truck instead of walking. How can we possibly carry everything all the way back?"

"It will be fine, you'll see. Remember, the more we use our muscles, the stronger they become. We will be fine, darling, don't you worry!"

His pipe was burning my favorite cherry flavor of tobacco; the sun was high, but not that strong now in winter that it burned our scalps; the breeze was fresh, and I could not be happier if I tried. As I thought about all the cooking, baking, and decorating all week in preparation for next Thursday's Christmas Eve feast, I was feeling quite euphoric. We arrived at the general store, and at once, the owner, Vincent, greeted us but with a look of pure agony. It was apparent to Papa and I, that he was busy running back and forth barking orders at his workers, answering customer requests, and generally managing things as if he were a *bull in a china shop*, as they say.

"Slow down, Vincent, everything will be okay," Papa said as we took a small metal, wheeled grocery cart from a line of them at the store's entrance.

"Only if I make it so," Vincent responded to Papa over his shoulder. He then turned to a worker bagging goods at the end of a queue of customers checking out at a register. "Use only two bags, not three!" he yelled. In his rush, his voice today seemed to me to be high-pitched and whiny, almost effeminate. Papa Ramon shook his head, and as we continued into the store, we heard Vincent hastily telling a customer, "Ma'am, they were fresh yesterday when our supplier delivered them. I doubt they could have soured overnight!"

We began carefully looking over the items on the shelves down the first aisle when Papa Ramon said to me, "Remember, darling, nothing is ever as urgent or important that you lose a respectful demeanor when it comes to handling *any of life's many trying circumstances.* Even though it may seem differently, it is a trap to believe that rushing around mindlessly and anxiously will ever help you get things done any quicker or better."

"Yes, Papa Ramon." We walked a few more steps down the aisle, and I chanced a criticism, something I had not customarily permitted myself to do. "This man Vincent seems like a silly man to me." As soon as I said it, I looked up at Grandpa to gauge his reaction.

"Yes, he is, and beware—you will run across many of them. But your assumption is correct, and I would advise that you never trust a man who throws away civility in order to exude self-importance."

I nodded and kept a reminder to myself about Papa's lesson. The store was crowded with many shoppers and their children. I recognized some friends from school and our neighborhood, and we would stop to chat now and then.

Papa Ramon took items we needed and deposited them into our cart. I noticed he did not seem overly bothered by the prices listed today, and so I finally asked him, "How are the prices today, Papa?"

"Not as good as I had hoped, but not as bad as I had feared."

With that response, I tried reconciling within my thoughts the effect our new leader, Batista, might be having on my family and neighbors; *insofar as the decisions he had made which had the power to influence pricing of goods in a store vital to their lives.* I had not heard bad things about him yet, and then again, I had not heard good things about him either. My curiosity finally getting the best of me, I asked Papa Ramon, "How is Batista doing so far as the leader of our government?"

"Good question, Angela!" Papa Ramon responded, making me feel proud that I had asked. I rolled the cart a little further down the aisle labelled as *Aisle 4* on a sign hanging from the ceiling. "He has appointed Miguel Mariano Gómez as our president, but everyone knows Batista is making all the decisions himself, and that this Miguel Gómez is there as just a puppet."

I laughed, beside myself, as I envisioned the mighty military man Batista pulling at strings with his hands to make this President Gómez dance and sway in front of large crowds, *as I did myself with my dolls, but without the strings and crowds*. I could not shake the image of this and continued laughing for a few more moments. Papa Ramon smiled as he looked down at me, somehow knowing just what was going through my mind.

"Yes, my sweet. Our mighty president is just a puppet! I have not yet come to a firm opinion about this Batista, but I must say, I am worried somewhat. I do not believe he is all he appears to be, and I am starting to feel that he does not have the true welfare of the Cuban people in his heart."

I stopped smiling and suddenly became apprehensive.

Papa Ramon recognized my change of mood. "Do not worry yourself. We Cubans are strong and resilient people. We have weathered many things—*corruption being one of them.* Each time someone comes to power who is not for us, we have someone else to rise up and chase them away!" I nodded. Papa Ramon grabbed a small burlap sack full of rice from off the shelf. I immediately recognized the blue label on its front and knew it came from one of our Western Provinces. "The only concern I see is that our citizens have to determine to find a leader once and for all who has no other intentions *but what is best for Cuba and its citizens.* That may seem like an easy thing to accomplish, but we have a history so far of choosing the wrong leaders, and I am not sure why that is."

I rubbed my nose as it itched from silt coming from the bags of flour we were now passing by. Papa's words had reminded me of my report at school and all the things I had read from that book on history I had used. I remembered something which had been posed by one of the articles, and which had perplexed me greatly. Once again now pondering what it had suggested, my concern grew, not only for our country, but for humanity itself. I now presented to Papa the crux of its message. "Perhaps it is because only bad people *greatly* desire to be in power to begin with, and they help one another to keep it; *and this prevents any of the good people to ever get the chance to be in control."*

Grandpa stopped in his tracks and thought about what I had said. Though I knew this had not been my original idea, at this point in time, I had wrestled with it long enough within myself that it had become my own. Papa looked down at me with a smile and nodded. "Very wise, my granddaughter, very wise!"

We had found everything we needed, which was a miracle in itself, seeing as how many people were preparing for the holidays. We came to the checkout lines, and we wound up in Vincent's line again, even though a few of the other lines were shorter. I believe Papa Ramon wound up in his line on purpose, and Vincent eyed us even with four customers ahead of us. Grandpa watched him the entire time we waited, as Vincent checked out the next three customers. The grocer would ask each of the customers, as it came their turn, "Hope you found everything you needed?" But he did not seem sincere, and it was just what he had learned to say as he greeted the next in line.

Finally, our turn came. As I unloaded the cart with our goods, Vincent looked up at Papa Ramon, but before he could use his line, Papa said, "Yes, we found everything we needed, thank you! How are you today?" But before Vincent could answer, Papa continued, "It's good to see the shelves stocked so fully, but I still think you are charging too much for most of the items."

Vincent kept on punching buttons on the register. Finally, he responded in a tone only a bit calmer than the one he had when we had first entered the store. "Ramon, I work hard keeping the shelves full by using the suppliers who can be relied upon to deliver goods on a regular basis. *It's nothing more than that.* If I used other suppliers, one week we might have enough varieties of flour, and the next we might only have one or two brands, and then only *in one-sized pouch.*"

Papa smiled and chuckled. "Well, I have to keep you honest. If that's what you say it is, then I have no choice but to believe you."

"You are always free to go to one of the other stores, though they are probably further away. *But do yourself and I both a favor* and at least go and price things. Then let me know what you find. If my prices are much higher, then you have the right to complain."

Papa took bills out of the wallet from his back pocket. He kept on looking at the grand total as Vincent was finishing ringing up the last items. "My problem is that I am too loyal, Vincent. I like coming here. I know where everything is, *and I can always give you a hard time* whenever I feel disposed to do as such."

Vincent smirked at Papa's joviality, and then Papa did too. They exchanged currency, and Vincent packed everything in four medium-sized bags, each of which was only half full. "You try and have yourself a great Christmas, with many blessings to you and your family," Papa said.

Vincent stopped for a complete moment. He looked at me and then Papa. "Thank you, Ramon. And to you and your family, the same."

Papa and I took a bag under each of our arms and departed. On the way home, Papa said, "Since the last time you were with me when we came to the store, I found out that Vincent *does charge* more than most other general stores, and it's not the government's policies, taxes, or delivery quotas that are causing it."

"What is it then, Papa?"

"He has a great big house and is adding to it to make room for his wife's parents to come and live with them."

"And that's why he's charging more, so he can make enough money to pay for the improvements to his house?"

"Yes." Somehow Papa managed to light his pipe once again while carrying his two bags. "But also, he donates money to charity, especially to an orphanage in Havana which had rescued him when he was a child on the streets with no family. I recently found out all this from a church friend of mine who has been friends with Vincent for twenty years."

I was shocked. I thought about what Papa had just said and then responded, "That's a very good thing he's doing then."

"Yes...but darling, the habit of feeling one deserves more from others than what is fair is never a good principle to allow for yourself. If many people succumbed to doing such, then the world would collapse beneath the weight of its own greed."

I knew what Papa had just said was absolute truth, and I vowed to myself then and there to never take advantage of others in any way. We kept on walking, and the bags, though cumbersome, were not unmanageable. As we got closer to the edge of town, we had one last stop to make. Up ahead was a man in a red and white striped outfit with a sailor's cap on top of his head. *It was quite a presence that he made.* He was a small man of middle age, thin, but with a gusto of personality. Shouting out for all to hear, he was saying, "Peanuts, get your peanuts here! And not only peanuts, but some of the freshest almonds anywhere to be found right off the tree!" Everyone knew him—it was Orillane, the street vendor with his peanut stand. He stood beside a large, wheeled metal cart with six drums of nuts, and there was a large red and white striped umbrella standing above both he and the cart.

"Who is this I see coming my way?" he asked as we approached. "Is that Ramon, the farmer, and his beautiful and darling granddaughter Angela come to keep him company on his shopping journey into town?"

I smiled, and Papa Ramon laughed as we came and stood beside the cart. "Orillane, how are you this fine day?" Papa asked.

"I am as fine and dandy as a soul could be, thanks for asking, and how might you be and your lovely granddaughter? And while I'm asking, how is the wife at home and your handsome boys, my friend Ramon?" He spoke a mile a minute, but his voice was warm, confident, and welcoming, and I immediately felt attracted to his robust mannerisms, as I always had from prior visits over the years.

"They are all doing just fine, and how about yours?" Papa asked.

"Well, with me as the head of the house, how could they not be as wonderful and joy-filled as the day they were born?"

Papa nodded and said, "Let us each try one of your almonds, Orillane. Mami is making her famous turrones, and we need the best you have."

As he selected two almonds from the bin with a metal scoop made for the occasion, he said, "I dare say, one each will not be enough. How about two?"

And with that, he presented the scoop with four large, shelled, and nutty almonds. We each took two, and I ate mine one at a time, but Papa put both in his mouth at the same time. Mine was sweet and nutty, tasting like sugar on the finest tree bark, and since I loved the smell of fresh wood, this was a high evaluation. The texture became smooth the more I chewed, and soon the almonds became like cream on my tongue. Papa was smiling as he swallowed, informing me he thought highly of the almonds as well. "Delicious—the best, as always. We'll take four bags!" He declared.

Orillane smiled and began scooping almonds into wax-covered white bags the size of a cantaloupe. When he had finished, he handed the bags to Papa, who divided them one each into the four bags we carried from Vincent's general store. Papa then handed Orillane some bills and said, "Merry Christmas, Orillane. Make it a good one and all the best to Yilian and the children."

"Thank you, Ramon! Merry Christmas, Ramon and Angela—*and to all!*" We started away, and Orillane called after us. "But, Ramon, your change!"

"No—keep it as a token of appreciation for all you do!" Papa said over his shoulder.

Twenty minutes later, we arrived home to see Abuela taking the fresh laundry down from the clothesline. As Papa put our items away, I went and helped her. "Did you enjoy your shopping expedition with Papa?"

"Yes, Abuela. It was great. I saw a lot of my friends and learned a bit about Vincent and his pricing habits. But I especially enjoyed seeing Orillane, who wishes you Merry Christmas by the way." I folded a towel and then took one of my own dresses from the line of clean clothes.

"Yes, he is a good man. He's been selling nuts at the same spot for twenty years now. Always remembers everyone by name, and many times their family members as well." Abuela checked to see if I had put the folded laundry into their correct piles.

"Abuela, when will we start the desserts?"

"First thing in the morning, darling." She smiled at me. "I hope you are fully prepared for the work to come!"

To me, it was not work. *I could not wait!*

I wound up staying over Papa and Abuela's house Sunday and Monday nights in addition to Friday and Saturday, as school was out for the holidays and Abuela had her hands full of flour, sugar, eggs, milk, and everything else going into dessert preparation. The remaining nights that week, I slept at home but came to my grand-parent's house first thing each morning.

I had remembered from years past some of the things Abuela needed me to do, but she was always right beside me offering guid-ance and instructions as we started. I beat eggs, measured cups of sugar, milk, rice, flour, and teaspoons of vanilla and baking soda. I ground cinnamon, chopped walnuts, pureed guava, mangos, and bananas. I stirred, blended, mixed, folded until my hands cramped and my arms felt like limp noodles. We separated egg whites, heated honey, candied citrus fruits, toasted almonds, and buttered and floured pans. All the while, cleaning as much as we could as we went along, but after each step of the process, there was always more to wash and dry, and how many times can one clean the same bowls and counters?

It was a long four-day weekend, but I did not mind at all. I had learned so much about food preparation along the way. When we had finished, there were dishes of pastelitos de guayaba, churros, and turrones, and then cupful servings of flan, arroz con leche, natilla, and cake platters of brazo de gitano and buñuelos de viento. We had to chase Juan away more than once; otherwise, he would try to sneak some of the finished, and sometimes some of the unfinished, good-ies. He made me laugh.

At one time, he said, *"But, Mami, you don't feed us enough, and I have to keep up my energy. Papo works us so hard!"*

Mateito was more diplomatic about it. *"Mami, just one, surely nobody will suffer hunger if I have just one to taste now. Besides, you do need someone to test to make sure it came out as perfectly delicious as you had hoped."*

Still, Abuela's answer to both was a consistent and firm, "No!" She told me in confidence that she occasionally and purposefully left a taste or two of things on the counter at night knowing they would each come in and take them. "However, if I gave in to their requests just one time, I would never have anything at all by Christmas Eve!"

Abuela and I spent the remainder of Tuesday unpacking five boxes of Christmas decorations. Papa Ramon had Mateito and Juan cut down a fresh pine tree and bring it into the house, where they stood it on a stand in the living room. Juan put Abuela's favorite Christmas albums on the turnstile, and we all worked hard for the next three hours adorning the tree, the front porch, a console table in the hall and one in the living room, and all of the front windowsills with decorations of garland, flowers, fixtures and ornaments, and of course, the manger, which stood on the mantle above the fireplace. It looked absolutely wonderful when we had finished, and we all sat in the living room tired from the day's preparations, admiring our handiwork.

On Wednesday, though I was already exhausted, *Papa Ramon reminded me we still had the tortas to make!* Honestly, I had forgotten all about them! It took us all afternoon, but we made all four batches. I vowed, for all to hear, that for the next two weeks I would not open another pouch of flour so long as I could help it! I returned home right before dinner. Having a few small bites of Mami's delicious ropa vieja, I immediately went to my bedroom, undressed, and laid down on my bed. Next thing I knew, it was Christmas Eve morning, and Mami and Papo were rustling to get everyone up and about and ready for the celebration! We all rushed to change into our casual clothes. Mami had us older children carry out the plates she had prepared along with presents, and we packed our newest baby brother Luis and all the rest of us into the truck and drove over to Abuela and Papa Ramon's. We could have easily walked, but with the baby and all the goods we were bringing, the truck was better.

Papo and Antonio helped Papa Ramon, Juan, and Mateito prepare the pits and fires for the two pigs to be roasted, while Abuela, Mami, Josephina, Aunt Lucia, Carmen, Maria, and I set the tables of food and dining outside in the backyard beneath the shade of several tall oak trees. The remainder of our guests began arriving—friends and neighbors and relatives—and I was even allowed to help to serve the drinks with alcohol, which were mostly beer and rum drinks mixed with coconut water, or one fresh juice or another. The pigs roasting and music filling the air with uplifting tunes, the younger children running around and playing, I looked at it all and thought *what a marvelous way to spend Christmas time!*

Everyone ate until content and then some. The food had all been delicious, but it was the wide array of desserts which stole the show. I tried not taking any credit for them, although Abuela insisted I did most of the work. The remaining gifts were opened and cherished, and all were in a jovial mood. Uncle Pablito finally arrived with Aunt Beatriz and cousin Caruca after spending most of the day with Uncle Pablito's family. I had been telling him about Vincent, since they both owned general stores. At one point, feeling enlivened by his interest in my reporting about our recent interactions with him, I began to imitate Vincent. I found myself putting on an old kitchen apron, and then standing tall and proud, in a squeaky and plaintive voice, I said, *"As are the prices I must pay for the goods in the first place!"* I then made believe I was looking at a customer and using the same voice, I said, *"Hope you found everything you needed?"* Continuing to another of Vincent's lines, I patted down my apron, then scratched my nose and barked out, *"Ma'am, they were fresh yesterday when our supplier delivered them. I doubt they could have soured overnight!"*

I had drawn the attention of almost everybody seated at the four tables around Uncle Pablito and me, and they were all laughing and smiling. I could not believe it as I looked up to see everyone was watching me. I did not know what to do next, and suddenly Antonio yelled out, "Do another one, Angela!" Instantly, I thought of the street vendor Orillane in his red and white striped outfit. I took off my apron, took Uncle Pablito's fedora from his head, and put it on my own. Smiling broadly, I called out in a rushed but friendly voice, *"Peanuts, get your peanuts here! And not only peanuts, but also the freshest almonds right off the tree! The best anywhere to be found!!"* I saw that I had everyone laughing again, and so I continued, *"I am as fine and dandy as a soul could be, thanks for asking, and how might you be and your lovely granddaughter? And while I'm asking, how is the wife at home and your handsome children and everyone in the whole world?"*

The crowd was roaring with laughter, and I loved it. Just like when I had given my report on history to my class, I was finding that having and holding the attention of a group of people due to my words or actions gave me a feeling of zest and comfort. *I enjoyed doing so, and somehow it all felt quite magical.*

We cleaned up what we had to and gave much food and dessert to everyone to take a share home with them. Tomorrow we would come back and finish eating, laughing, and cleaning up, but now it was time for us to prepare for Midnight Mass. Giving kisses and hugs, we said goodbye to those we would not see at church, and then we made our way home. Washing up and changing, we were ready to go by 11:20 p.m.

Each of us ladies in our finest dresses with a white mariposa flower in our hair, and the gentlemen in their finest suits and shoes, we all managed to squeeze into one of Papo's trucks and made our way to church in time for Midnight Mass. I adored our church—*Our Lady of Sorrows*—and it always took my breath away walking on to the terrace in front of the building itself, just knowing I was about to enter God's own dwelling place. The church had been built in the 1860s and had two bell towers, one on each front corner, and four majestic pillars which stood tall, out about five meters in front of the church's entrance. The building was all white, with a bronze-colored trim running around its entire perimeter and in eight wide columns, two to a side, going from the top to bottom. During Sunday morning masses, once inside the church one noticed immediately the sunlight streaming through large stained-glass windows, each of them depicting a scene from Jesus's struggles during the passion, gracing the entire interior of the church. The colorful light played gently with a quiet elegance over all of the statues, the altar, the pews, and vestibule. Tonight, in lieu of sunlight, we had the soft warm glow of flickering candlelight coming from candelabras spread across the church. I had come to love the statue of Our Lady standing upright in the right corner, beside the altar. Her eyes exuded both a desperate love and pity at the same time. Mami had explained to me years before that her expression bore love for Jesus and pity for mankind.

We took one complete row, and I noticed Aunt Beatriz, Uncle Pablito, and Caruca sitting two pews ahead of us. They saw us and waved hello, and we all waved back. We saved room in our pew for Abuela, Papa Ramon, Juan, and Mateito, who arrived a few minutes after us, and they nodded their greeting, but right away kneeled to say prayers before mass. I looked for Pilar and her parents, but they were sometimes lazy about attending services, and when they had not arrived by five minutes until midnight, I assumed they would miss. Just before mass began, Aunt Lucia, her husband, Juan, and my cousins Carmen and Maria came into the church. They had to take seats all the way at the back since now the church was full. The choir began, and as the first hymn filled the air with the love of God, it was their soulful and harmonic voices which lifted us briefly to heaven.

The pastor was Padre Jorge Sebastiano, and he had an ease with words that went along with his loving and gentle disposition. For me, this made all his masses somehow joyous, but especially this Christmas Evening Mass. At one point, my youngest sister Estrella, now two, became bored and began kicking at the pew in front of us, possibly trying to get the attention of the little boy sitting there with his parents. Papo never had patience with any of us misbehaving in public, where he always insisted on our best behavior, but now especially in church. He immediately grabbed Estrella firmly by the wrist and pointed his finger at her sternly. She would never do anything but listen attentively and sit calmly during mass from then on.

When mass finished, we greeted everyone outside and wished Merry Christmas to all. When I put my head down on my pillow that night, I had such an exuberant feeling of peace, love, and faith in God. We had such joyful and loving family, friends, and neighbors, and we had been blessed to be able to share our fortunes with those we loved. *What more could one ask than that?*

Chapter Three

Funny how world events can change one's plans definitively and permanently, despite a lifetime of preparation. Secondary school for me was spent while the world was at war for the second time in as many decades. Uncertainty, fear, and necessity led every citizen around the world to forget about planning for a future and to concentrate one's efforts at surviving and getting by with the essentials one needed for their existence. Nazis were everywhere in the form of soldiers and spies, and none of the world's leaders took for granted at first who were their allies and who were their foes.

With the 1940 elections, our military leader and chief, Fulgencio Batista, was finally made our president. At first, there was much uncertainty about whether he would align Cuba with the Axis or the Allies. The US watched him very closely. Shortly after he became president, Batista immediately legalized a pro-fascist organization which had ties to Spain. He then sent the British a large quantity of sugar as a gift and suggested to the United States that the two countries unite to launch a joint US-Latin American invasion of Spain intent to overthrow dictator Franco and his regime. Batista finally and officially threw his support to the Allied cause in February 1941, when he ordered all German and Italian consular officials to leave our country. Cuba entered the war on December 9, 1941, by declaring war on Japan after the devastating attack on the United States Navy base at Pearl Harbor, Hawaii, just two days earlier. Batista then declared war on Germany and Italy on December 11, 1941. Mami often commented on our alliance with the US, and she was happy that we had them on our side. I knew it made her feel safer knowing we did.

Still, we worried constantly just how far the Germans would go, and if their boats, submarines, and aircraft would be so bold as to attack our country. Meanwhile, Batista looked to dispel persistent rumors, later proven false, that the Germans were operating small bases hidden in coves along Cuba's coast to resupply their U-boats even though German supply submarines did come through the waters surrounding our nation. He signed a mutual defense pact with Mexico so that the two countries could defend against enemy submarines in the Gulf of Mexico. Fear had been in the air for well over four years as nobody could say with any certainty that we were safe, or if the Germans would send missiles and bombs our way, especially on our island, which was detached from most of our mainland Navy bases. Altogether, Cuba had lost 10,296 tons of shipping during the war, as well as about eighty lives, including those of a dozen or so American armed guards.[1]

By 1946, we were starting to get our lives somewhat back to normal after the war, even though I believe after experiencing such a major event as that war had been, there would never be anything close to normal ever again. It changed people and disrupted forever the course their lives would have taken had it never happened. As Papa Ramon had said long ago, Cubans are resilient people, and so one way or the other, we went forward. Now that I had finished school, I was helping Mami with her dress and tailoring business. Antonio and Fernando had gone to work with Papo full-time driving trucks to supply the lumberyard with fresh trees and then to distribute and deliver the lumber to customers. Josephina was now helping at Aunt Beatriz and Uncle Pablito's general store where she stocked shelves and rang up sales. She also had a growing interest in helping Caruca, who had developed the area of the store set aside for clothing, shoes, and jewelry into its own upscale boutique. Always dressed in finest fashion, Josephina was becoming quite business-minded, just like our cousin Caruca. My friend Pilar was staying these past years with relatives in Bejucal, as it was thought to be a safer location to survive the war. Nobody could tell when she might return home.

---

[1] https://en.wikipedia.org/wiki/Cuba_during_World_War_II

Finally, the youngest three of our siblings were still in school. Lilliana would be through with school at the end of May, and yet of all of us, it had been Lilliana who had excelled the most during the past several years.

As accomplished as I had become making dresses and helping Mami with the tailoring needs of her business, my heart was never committed to it. Lilliana, on the other hand, had a gift for this work and would be described as having an innate genius when it came to inventing clothing for both men and women. Her designs had exploded in popularity and had attracted a very robust following of clients for the past three years. By the time she turned fourteen, she could not keep up with the demands for her clothing, and so Mami and I helped her where we could. Though she wanted to leave school before graduating to pursue her clothing business full-time, Papo insisted she finish.

One Saturday in early May, Fernando was driving me into town as he occasionally did since at this time, I still had not bothered to learn how to drive on my own. He was making good money with Papo, and he and I had grown close over the past years. For some reason, I had taken on the role of surrogate mother to him since Mami had been so busy with the younger children when he was going through formative years. Truth be told, I loved him possibly more than I did my other siblings. Something about his blond hair and blue eyes, his happy demeanor, and his absolute concern that others be filled with joy so long as he could help it, attracted me to him as if he were my special little charge. Now, not so little anymore, I enjoyed going through the growing years together with him. He did not seem to have much of an interest in girls or dating just yet; however, he realized that I had taken an interest in young men, and though not jealous, I would say Fernando had grown protective of me.

"Sis, why don't we make a stop at Rudolfo's Candy Shop?"

I had a late growing spurt and was always hungry, and Fernando knew my weakness for fancy candies, confections, and fine chocolates. For his part, Fernando always could eat, and we were forever amazed how trim and fit he remained despite his ravenous consumption of almost every edible thing. Now that I was nineteen and had just recently outgrown most of my own clothes, Mami suggested I buy new dresses and blouses since we had enough with making everything for all of our collective clientele. Fernando loved helping me choose things and would toss in the extra money when necessary so that I could get some of the more expensive clothing. I knew Fernando also very much enjoyed going to Rudolfo's to see what new and tasty items they had made or had imported for the week. I would not disappoint him.

"Well, I suppose if you insist on going, we might just pop in for a bit to say hello to Rudy and his lovely wife, Christiana."

He smiled knowing I was looking forward to seeing the new displays as much as he. "Since the war is over, Papo is busier than ever. I had a good week, and money isn't meant to last forever after all." He looked at me with his gorgeous face, and as I usually did, I could not help but think he was going to make some woman very happy one day.

"Still, Fernando, it would not hurt you to save some of your earnings for whenever you might need to support someone you will eventually fall in love with, and maybe to get a house of your own one day." I dared a stern glance in his direction. We had just entered the outskirts of town along the main avenue. I could see already the streets close to downtown were crowded with shoppers, stands, cars, and wagons.

"Yes, perhaps you are right. Although, I would also admit there is an equal chance that I could remain single for quite some time. I see no rush in the matter and am happy to be living at home still with Papo, Mami, and the family." Sometimes, I just could not figure out my brother and lately had given up trying. He had a mind and direction all his own and, so far, had fulfilled absolutely nobody's expectations of what course either might take. "Seems to me, you and Josephina are the ones headed towards finding husbands and moving on to families of your own!" As he said this, I detected a slight bit of longing in his voice, or perhaps it had been fear of being left behind.

"Oh, I don't know, Fernando. Love seems to be the farthest thing on my mind." Although his statement was meant to be lighthearted, for some reason, it brought me a feeling of uncertainty. Like my brother, some part of me felt no need to rush to be moving out of my home in order to start one of my own. Another part of me, a growing one at that, did feel restless and in need of companionship that went beyond friends and the family I had always known. Josephina had been dating a man for two years now, and we all expected one day soon, she would announce that they had engaged and intended to marry. On the other hand, Antonio seemed content to date and chase one woman after another with no serious intent for any of them. I could feel Fernando's eyes watching my face in order to see if I was going to give anything away regarding my hopes for the future. I turned to him. "You know, it's not easy to figure all of this stuff out."

As he pulled Papo's pickup truck into a parking spot adjacent to Rudolfo's Candies, he smirked and shook his head slightly. "I say the time is coming soon for both you and Josephina to find a permanent man with whom you will want to start a family. It's just how it goes—besides, we have too many women in the house as it is. Not that I don't want you to stay. Heck, I don't want to give away my best sis in the whole world. What will I do with myself besides work then?"

I smiled and shook my head. "You know if and when the time comes, my husband will have to agree that you and you alone are welcome to our house and for any meal you would like without an invitation."

As he opened the driver's side door to depart the truck, he looked back one more time. "Thanks, sis—you know I'm going to be always checking up on you to make sure you are okay and that he is treating you like you deserved to be treated."

I opened the passenger door. "Yes, Fernando, that will be my expectation, and without it, I don't think I would ever feel safe in marriage no matter if he were the Pope himself!"

Fernando scrunched up his face. "Popes can't marry."

"Well, it just shows you. He had better be a good man and take care of his loved ones." With that, I slammed the door closed, and Fernando, shaking his head, met me on the sidewalk and we walked into Rudolfo's.

The sweet aromas of freshly made candies met our noses like a field of wildflowers on a spring day. We became like children again as we hopped from one bin to the next in a frenzy of fascination.

"Good afternoon, Angela and Fernando!" Rudy said to us from behind the main counter of the store, which was painted bright pink. His wife popped her head from the doorway to the back kitchen, greeting us with a smile and a warm welcome. "Try one of these, my darlings." Rudy met us in the middle of the store with two large candies on a napkin. They were two round wafers of chocolate filled with a gooey coconut mixture in the middle. The chocolate had crushed nuts in it and the coconut was so fresh, we could see the fresh grated white meat sticking out from the stack.

Fernando took one first and bit it carefully. I watched him as he chewed before taking the second from Rudy's hand. Immediately, his eyes grew wide and engaged. His face became pure radiance as he continued chewing and then swallowed. "This is why this trip into town is worth it for us each week. You and Christiana are artists, but not just any kind of artist—you are both virtuosos whose works are masterpieces!"

I bit my piece knowing the taste could not possibly live up to my brother's raves. As I chewed, I knew at once I was wrong. The texture was perfection as the shredded coconut met the bits of almonds and cashews in just the right crunch as the chocolate and remainder of the coconut mixture coalesced into a smooth, sweet, and savory delicacy as it slipped down the palate. I was in heaven! Finally swallowing with both men smiling at my own amazed enjoyment of the candy, I said to Rudy, "I don't know who thought of this, you or Christiana, but it is surely the finest candy ever to grace my lips. I must bring Abuela and Papa Ramon a whole bagful, and then we will need two bags at home at least."

"What do you call these?" Fernando asked.

Christiana came through the kitchen door shouting out, "I call them perlas de coco!" She had a white apron on, her hair tied in a bun, and looked happy.

Rudy, who was shorter than his wife, was dressed in his brown business suit as usual. He said, "Yes, that is what we call them!"

Christiana rolled her eyes as she came to greet us with yet another new confection. "Here, these are just finished. Try one." She extended her hand out with two clear rock candies the color of bright pink coral.

Fernando and I each plucked one into our mouths. The taste was of both cinnamon and mango, with a hint of vanilla. Creamy and succulent, as I allowed the candy to melt in my mouth, it made me want to close my eyes as I envisioned myself lying in a field of grass on a beach by the ocean.

Needless to say, we left the store with eight bags altogether. Rudy had packed a bag with ice inside the larger bag, so the candies did not melt in the heat of the day. We spent the next two hours at three clothing stores, and after trying on various shirts, blouses, dresses, pants, and shoes, we had between us four bags of clothing.

Driving home elated from our day's work, Fernando said, "I am ravished. Hand me just one more perla de coco!"

I took two out of the inside bag. "You're going to spoil your appetite for Mami's dinner!"

He looked at me as if to say, "You've got to be joking."

We stopped by Abuela and Papa Ramon's on the way home and dropped off two bags of mixed goodies. Abuela tried one of the confections, and immediately her eyes drew open wide and she smiled. "Those two always did make the best candy. Sorry to say, because over the years I've tried honing my skills and outdoing their products, but I must admit it is of no use."

"There, there, my sweet," Papa Ramon said. We had all gathered at the kitchen table. Both Juan and Mateito had married and moved out, leaving just my two grandparents in the large house. "You are sweet enough and are like candy to those who love you, so why must you prepare confections when *you are one*—the best one of them all!" He stood and went behind Abuela, wrapping his arm around her chest and kissing her on top of the head. Abuela smiled and patted him gently on his arm.

"Those two have been in love for almost their entire lives," Fernando said as we drove home. "We should be so lucky to find spouses whom we will love as much in fifty years as we had the first day we met."

He was right, and I knew the wisdom in his words. "Correct you are, brother of mine. Do you think they still make them like they had when our grandparents and parents got together?"

"I'm not quite sure about that, sis. But we have to hope they do for our own sakes."

Papo and our siblings were just getting seated for dinner when we arrived home. We had arrived home later in the day than we had expected, but nobody fussed. Estrella and Luis could not wait to see what were in the white bags from Rudolfo's Candies, but we insisted they had to wait until after dinner.

"It's not fair," Luis protested. "You got to have some at the store and on the way home, I bet!"

Estrella liked having a comrade-in-arms to support a viewpoint which she favored, and she chimed in. "Agreed! I think we should each be able to choose one candy right now before Mami serves dinner!"

Papo looked at Estrella with an expression of mock chagrin. "No and no again! Mami worked long and hard preparing dinner and would feel utterly disappointed should her meal be substituted with candy. Albeit, wonderful, delicious, mouth-watering candy, but worthless sweets nonetheless!"

With that, Luis heard his cue and went into complete drama modality. If I had not mentioned it before, Luis had become quite the comedian of the family as the years had unfurled. Now he stood from his chair and brought both his hands to his heart. "But, Papo, please! Please, Papo, what will it take for a young boy to get just a small taste of something as you just described so absolutely and fantastically out-of-this-world with flavor and yumminess?" He looked across the dining room to make sure he had all of our attention. Suddenly, he swept both his arms outward in grand fashion and began shaking his hands as we had seen the dancers from TV doing. He swooped and spun, then shimmied and gyrated his hips. "Papo, look—I have broken out in song and dance and have done so gladly if that is what it will take to move you to grant permission for us poor, starving children the grace of a single candy." Just as I was thinking *perhaps dance, but where was the song?* Luis suddenly opened his mouth and actually quite melodically, to the tune of Ernesto Lecuona's "Always in My Heart" (from the film of the same name), sang out the words "Papo, Papo, you must understand my belly aches for just one taste…if you will just see, how much it would mean to me, I will kiss you and hug you as much as you want, just say the word…"

Just then Mami came from the kitchen carrying two casserole dishes full, and she joined his song in melody, but with these words, "My son, if you don't sit right now, you had better run…because when I am through with you," she scrunched up her face in exaggerated anger and finished by singing out, *"it will be no fun!"*

We all burst out laughing and then helped Mami bring in the rest of the dishes as Luis smiled and plopped down into his seat.

"I think you laid it on a bit too thickly," Estrella said to him.

He reached over and pinched her on the cheek, to which she brushed his hand away and then to our surprise, said, *"Not at the dinner table, Luis, please! Where's your manners?"*

Over the next few months, the summer grew hot and then even more fiercely hot, and it seemed we all had all we could do to try keeping cool enough to bring a bit of comfort from day to day. Abuela needed some ointments, bandages, and gauze for the farmworkers, as she was the nurse to Papa Ramon's crew. Mami also needed lotions, and I had been wanting to try out one of their new perfumes. The pharmacy was north of town, close to Uncle Pablito and Aunt Beatriz's store, but I was looking for an excuse to go into town anyway, and so I volunteered to make the trip by bus. My sister Josephina could easily have gone after work, but as I had said, I wanted to go just to get away from the house for an afternoon and to try out the perfumes anyway.

Funny how changing one's schedule just for an afternoon could make all the difference in the world as to one's fate. Just before I had boarded the bus, Aunt Lucia came to me trotting from her house.

"Angela, I heard from your Mami that you were going to the pharmacy." I nodded, and she reached into her pocket to take out some bills. "I need this medicine for Uncle Juan's stomach, which has been sour now for a few days." She unrolled the bills, and there was a small slip of paper with the name of a new stomach remedy. I looked at it and recognized what she was looking for since Papo had used it after the holidays. "I have been told they have it now, and it's back in stock. They had been out of it last week when I was there."

"Sure, Aunt Lucia, I can get that for you while I am there." I took the bills and paper from her hand.

"Thank you, sweetheart. Uncle Juan will be so thankful that you were able to get it on your trip."

Just then the bus pulled up along the side of the main avenue. As I stepped up onto the stairs leading inside, I turned back and said, "I will come by the house as soon as I get back."

She nodded and waved at me as I paid my fare and took a seat. The bus was half full, and all the windows were open. Still, it was hot and stuffy inside. The rhythm of the movement, along with the engine's moderate humming, made me sleepy, and I dozed on and off along the way. We travelled through town, and I was happy to see everyone busy going about their chores and getting the things they needed. It took another fifteen minutes on the bus, with about five stops, to get to the north part of town, but we finally arrived, and I pulled the cord signaling I wished to depart. Before standing up, I checked my hair in my reflection in the window and saw that it was not too bushy as it could get sometimes with the humidity and hot ocean breezes. I had used some of Josephina's hair spray before having left, and now considered that perhaps if I had enough money, that I should buy a can of my own.

I was wearing the yellow dress I had made myself after one of Lilliana's designs, and I thought I looked quite respectable. Also, the bonnet I had put on helped my overall appearance, and I considered that I could pass as a young woman, maybe even one who worked in a store, or even a professional office. I felt like a million bucks as I walked along the avenue for several blocks toward the pharmacy. Many boys and men gazed at me, a few nodded at me as I passed and gave me a wanton smile. I did not want to mislead any of them, and so I held a generous smile on my face but otherwise kept my eyes staring down at the ground in front of me. As I approached the store, I noticed a shoeshine stand just adjacent to the pharmacy's front door. There was a man sitting in the chair getting his shoes shined by a boy of about fourteen who kneeled on the ground as he used a cloth with polish on it to buff the top of the man's black shoes, which looked like they were still brand-new. The man was reading a paper, and his head was pointed away from my approach.

As I rounded the stand to make my way to the front door, suddenly the paper lowered from his face, and I get a glimpse of the man for the first time. My heart skipped a beat upon seeing him since he was absolutely gorgeous. He had deep brown eyes with neatly cropped, thick eyebrows, the most exquisitely chiseled cheeks and well-defined cheekbone I had ever seen, and a thin mustache above his top lip which complimented his appearance and somehow gave him the look of a movie star from one of those Hollywood movies. He wore a black fedora and business suit, and he smiled immediately when our eyes met. Neither of us said a word to the other; however, there was an unexplained feeling of communication between us. The air electrified, and all the sounds, sights, and activity around us came to an immediate stop. I continued on into the store with an elation thus far unknown in my life. *Oh well, how silly of me—surely, I will never see him again.*

Forgetting all about him, I took a handheld cart from the stand and went about shopping for the items I had come for, but still my mind felt burdened. Some part of me wanted to introduce myself to this man and strike up a conversation, although I would not know what to say or even why I felt this way. Having success finding the rest of the items on my list, I went and tried a few fragrances at the perfume counter. I found one I fell in love with and looked to see it was named simply *Cherry Blossom.* I decided not to buy the can of hairspray this time around as I had a lot to carry already. I paid for my things and retrieved a medium-sized bag and then made my way to the front door.

A man with his two little boys beside him held the door for me as I made my way out. Although I tried not showing it, my eyes almost popped out of my head as I saw the man still sitting in the chair, conversing with the shoeshine boy even though the work had been done. Immediately, he jumped out of the chair and approached me.

"It is a blessing from God himself that I have found you here," he said. His voice was deep, confident, and calm all at the same time, as if he had practice using it for important announcements. However, it was his gaze upon me that was most captivating. His large brown eyes shined a soulful spirit, and though he did not know me, I felt his love showering me, emitting from him like blazing flames from a warm fire on a cold night.

He was irrepressible and walked beside me as I made my way down the sidewalk. "My name is Ricardo, and I want you to know you are the most beautiful woman I have ever had the pleasure of laying my eyes upon. I was meant to meet you here today outside this pharmacy, and though you don't know it just yet, I am correct when I say we were destined to be together forever."

I was beside myself, with many different feelings running through me all at once. I turned to look at him as we walked, and though his words had been confident, he seemed somewhat meek and humble as I took a full view of him. "Is that so?" I said, the only words that I found could easily tumble out of my mouth at the time.

"It is so."

We continued walking, and I realized I could either choose to have a proper conversation or could tell him *no thanks* and leave him behind. I remembered how I had felt when I first saw him while entering the pharmacy, and that I had felt inclined then to go back out and talk with him. Call me many things, but foolish is not one of them. I stopped in my tracks, and then turned to him. "And, Ricardo, just what is it that you do with yourself and how do I know you are not some evil man trying to persuade me to have a night of fun at both of our expenses?"

"Well, darling, let me start out by assuring you that I am an upright and civil man whose only intent is proving to the woman before me that I am her man." He took off his hat and just then

I turned and glanced into the street only to see my Aunt Beatriz and Uncle Pablito driving by in their automobile. Both gave me a stern glance as they passed. Though this distracted me momentarily, Ricardo continued, and I was soon engaged once again in our conversation. "You see, I currently work as floor manager at a bottling company called Campa in Pinar Del Río." He saw the look on my face—Pinar Del Río was on the mainland, about a three-hour drive from the port of Batabanó, where the ferry boat from Isle of Pines landed. "But wait," he continued, "my family has a home here on Isle of Pines, in the northeastern part of Santa Fe, and I have an internship at the University in Nueva Gerona as a professor in agriculture. You see, I have a college degree in agriculture but am now attending the doctorate program in pedagogy at the University of Pinar Del Río. My hope is to become a professor and teach at the collegiate level, and I can surely do that here in Nueva Gerona if I so desire."

All of this suddenly seemed so uncertain to me, and I wandered over to the bench along the street beneath a tall cottonwood tree. Sitting down upon it, Ricardo came and sat beside me. "Don't let a bit of this bother you, my dear. Let us get to know one another, and you will see there can be no other man for you than me. Come, let us go wherever you had been heading before I interrupted you. We can talk as we do so." He stopped for a moment and scratched his head. "Where was it that you were headed?"

I looked at his eyes once again. His sincerity was refreshing, and somehow, I found myself hopelessly trusting this man and his words. It would be easy enough to find out about him and if he were a doctoral student, an adjunct professor at the university in Nueva Gerona, and I also considered that if his family lived in that part of Santa Fe, even part time, surely my aunt and uncle would know of them. I admit, I was taken by him and hoped for the best. "I am due to take the bus back to my aunt's house, which must be close to your house, in order to deliver medicine, and then head to my home several blocks away."

"Well, see, that is fine. I am taking the same bus home myself. Allow me to accompany you."

Once again, I did not know what to say. However, it seemed likely that one way or the other we would wind up on the same bus. "Perhaps that would be okay," I answered.

We sat beside one another on the bus, and I told Ricardo about my family, the farm, my papo's business. He discussed that his papo worked all his life running a tobacco farm in Pinar Del Río and that he had a large family with four brothers and three sisters. His father was originally from Las Palma Islas Canarias and his mami from Andalusia, Spain. While the rest of his siblings remained working on the farm, only he and his sister Manuela had finished school and gone on to college. He told me his family was poor when he was a small child and often he could only take a sweet potato to school for lunch, and that is why he had wanted to get his doctorate degree and become a professor, so that he would be able to sufficiently provide for his future wife and children in a better fashion than he himself had.

We had talked so much that the bus ride went quickly. He asked for my address once we departed the bus, but I said no, I could not give that to him. Anyway, I let him walk me up until a block from Aunt Lucia's and then said goodbye to him. He seemed crestfallen that I did not commit to another meeting or promise of getting together soon. Still, I had learned from Papa Ramon that things should not be rushed, and good men would always find a way to fulfill their purposes. He did take my hand before leaving me at the corner, and he gently kissed it before nodding, turning, and walking toward his home.

I was filled with uncertainty for the next few days. Perhaps I should have told him I would meet him at a café at a given day and time. I thought of his smile, his sincerity, and most of all, those beautiful brown eyes so full of spirit and soul.

"You seem distracted," Mami said to me one afternoon as we sewed together. I did not tell her about meeting Ricardo just yet. I waited, but so far, it seemed neither Aunt Beatriz or Uncle Pablito had said anything to Papo about seeing me talking with Ricardo on the street in town.

Early the following week, I made a trip into town—this time, I walked all the way since it was a cooler day—for two reasons. First of all, I wanted to stop by church to leave a donation for the poor of our parish from my pay helping Mami and Lilliana. Secondly, I had hoped to catch Aunt Beatriz at home to discuss what she felt about this man Ricardo, seeing she and Uncle Pablito had already noticed our conversing and so far had kept quiet about it. My mind was still spinning with my thoughts and conjectures about him. My heart, however, would not leave him alone.

As I came out from the church after leaving my contribution in the collection box by the petition candles and saying some prayers to Our Lady, I felt better than I had and told myself no matter what happened as for my romance, it was all in God's hands and his will. *Wouldn't you know it?* Coming around the corner two blocks from my aunt's house, I saw a man walking toward me *and knew right away it was Ricardo.* His smile blazed as he stepped up his pace.

When he was within three meters from me, he said, "My darling, what a pleasant surprise!"

I could not for the life of me figure out how he had found me, but it did not matter. I was happy to see him. "I would say you were following me, Ricardo, if I did not know any better."

We stood before each other for a moment, gazing into each other's eyes. "No—it is fate, my sweet. I was on my way to church to drop off a donation, as I always do this time each week when I am here. And where might you be heading off to on such a fine day?"

"To my Aunt Beatriz's house just down the block here." I had taken a chance of giving away a relative's residence but did not care.

"Well, let me escort you there. Church will be open all day." He crooked his arm, expecting me to put mine within, which I did.

We began walking, and this would be the first time in my life I had a man's affection besides from family. The feeling it allowed was tremendous, as if the whole world had just opened to endless possibilities. We walked, and I remained elated, although I did not know what I would do once we arrived at Aunt and Uncle's. I knew they had taken off today from the store to let Caruca run the place, as they decided working every day all day was not a good thing for the soul.

My heart skipped a beat as we approached their house. Uncle Pablito was out in the front yard working in the flower bed there, and he looked up and immediately saw us. He stood and examined our coupling, and then pointed right away at the front door. *"Angela, may I have a word with you?"*

I stopped in my tracks and unhooked my arm from Ricardo. "Oh, dear." I did not know what I should do.

"Go, Angela. Talk with your uncle and aunt. I will wait here for you. Once you are done, come out and tell me all about what they said."

Looking into his eyes, I knew he would remain steadfast on the spot. I nodded, then turned and walked to the front door. Both Uncle Pablito and Aunt Beatriz were there waiting for me. They welcomed me inside, and Uncle closed the door behind me. We at once sat in the living room—I on the small sofa and Aunt and Uncle across from me on the larger couch. They were both dressed in casual clothes, suggesting a day out in the yard.

Aunt Beatriz began. "Darling, who is this man, and how long have you been seeing him?"

Before I could answer, Uncle Pablito said, "I know who he is—Ricardo Gomez and his family have a house in Northeast Santa Fe. They are a family of farmers from Pinar Del Río, although he and his sister Gladys earn extra money by selling clothes out of the house here."

"Yes, that is true. Ricardo is earning his doctorate in pedagogy and will one day be a professor." I turned to Aunt Beatriz. "And we have not been dating. Actually, this is only the second time I have seen him, and the first was when you saw us in passing downtown."

"Have you told your papo and mami about him?" He did not wait for me to answer. "I know his kind, Angela," Uncle Pablito went on. "He is a womanizer and only wants to use you and then go on to someone else."

I felt hurt and betrayed. Something told me Uncle was incorrect, but I could not be sure.

Aunt Beatriz was laughing for some reason. "If he is a womanizer, then he is a real man, of that I can assure you."

We sat silent for a moment.

"It's best not to hide things like this from your parents," Uncle said. "Regardless of who he is, you must let them know you have found an interest in someone."

Aunt Beatriz sat up. "Why don't you invite him here to our house this evening. We can chaperone you while you get to know each other. Your parents would feel better this way, and you won't have to worry about them snooping around as you spend time together."

This seemed reasonable to me. I saw Uncle Pablito was nodding his head in approval of this plan of action. *Now, would Ricardo go along with it?* Believing I did not have much choice, I agreed and then stood. They both watched from the door as I made my way back to him.

I told him what they hoped we could do going forward from here, and he smiled immediately. "I will return tonight at seven, how is that?"

I said, "Fine. Seven it is!"

He looked over to Aunt and Uncle at the front door and waved jubilantly at them. I turned, and Aunt Beatriz was smiling and waving back, but Uncle Pablito remained rigid and stern. I said, *"Okay, then I shall see you then, my angel."*

He kissed the back of my hand and nodded, turned, and then departed down the block to the church presumably.

Chapter Four

I had arrived at my uncle and aunt's house about ten minutes to seven. Dressed in my finest lavender dress with a white lily adorning the right cross strap, I wondered if I had overdressed for the occasion. My hair was, as customary, quite curly, and lengthy in the back, and I had on a bit of makeup—mostly rouge, and I had used my favorite shade of pink lipstick to highlight my lips. Of course, I had also dabbed on some of my newest perfume.

"You look stunning," Aunt Beatriz said, smiling, as I came into the living room and sat on the larger of the two couches. I figured best to have Ricardo and I on the large couch so that we would not be tempted to sit too close together. I smiled nervously as she straightened out some items on the bookshelf along the interior wall.

Uncle Pablito came in with his newspaper and sat on the sofa. He and Aunt Beatriz had dressed a bit more formally—he in dress slacks and turquoise guayabera, and she in a soft white dress.

"What did you tell your parents?" he asked as he began opening the newspaper.

I was aware this was a test. I had only told them I was going to Aunt and Uncle's to help them with sorting a box of new clothing which had just come in from Spain and which Caruca was going to sell at the store. As I hesitated, in search of a response, Aunt Beatriz came to my rescue.

"I hope you just told them you were coming for a visit. It's too early to worry them about a boyfriend. If this does not go well and you decide to never see him again, it's best they don't even know." I felt grateful for her intervention, even as Uncle Pablito shook his head with a slight nonplussed expression adorning his face.

Aunt Beatriz went into the kitchen, and uncertain what to do next, I sat silently with my hands on my lap. Uncle Pablito began reading his newspaper, and a moment later, Aunt Beatriz returned with two cups of fresh chilled coconut water with lime wedges. She put these down on the coffee table between the two couches and then went over to the Victrola. I looked at the clock on the wall, and it showed just about a minute before seven. Soon, music began coming from the record player, and I recognized that Aunt Beatriz had put on the album with some of my favorite Cuban love songs.

Suddenly, there was a knock on the door, and my heart skipped a beat. Aunt Beatriz turned around from the Victrola and glanced at me with an apprehensive smile as she went to the front door. When she opened it, Ricardo was there and greeted her with a huge smile of his own and a bouquet of fresh flowers.

"Very good evening to you," he said. He looked stunning to me, dressed in a light gray business suit, shiny black shoes, and blue tie. His hair was combed back and had the look of being just washed and coifed with styling gel, but it was his smile along with that handsome and rugged jawline which stood out most of all and gave his presence intense character. He must have made quite an appearance because Aunt Beatriz stared him up and down for a moment longer than necessary before she ushered him into the living room.

Uncle Pablito barely nodded at Ricardo over his newspaper as my aunt had him take a seat on the couch beside me.

"I'll be right back," she said, and then she scuttled into the kitchen.

I could feel my heart pounding loudly and quickly in my chest when Ricardo glanced at me. Attempting to smile so as not to give away the feelings of trepidation I was feeling, I crossed my legs and gazed into his beautiful brown eyes. Our eyes locked for a long moment before he said, "My darling, you are as beautiful as ever." He then moved a wisp of hair that had fallen across my eyes. "As beautiful as ever a woman was *or could be.*" He took my hand into his and then slowly bowed his head to plant a loving and gentle kiss. I was enamored by this act and became lost in a moment of utter bliss. That is, until I heard Uncle Pablito *quite obnoxiously* clearing his throat. Ricardo quickly withdrew his hand from mine and sat upright, and then Aunt Beatriz returned with his flowers in a vase, and she put them down in the middle of the coffee table. Looking first at the flowers, Ricardo then turned his attention to the two cups there. He asked, "Are one of these for me?"

Aunt Beatriz answered affirmatively, and Ricardo lifted the one closest to him to his lips and sipped. "Ah, delicious and refreshing!" He smiled at Aunt Beatriz and said, "Thank you..." Suddenly, his smile disappeared, and his face took on a concerned countenance.

Realizing he did not know how he should address each of them, Aunt Beatriz said, "Mr. and Mrs. Martinez."

Nodding, Ricardo smiled once again and responded, "Thank you, Mrs. Martinez."

"What kind of work do you do?" Uncle Pablito asked without looking up from whatever had earned his interest in the newspaper.

Ricardo put the cup of coconut water back down onto the table and cleared his throat. "Well, I hope to one day be a professor at the university here in Isle of Pines. Right now, I am attending the doctorate program for pedagogy in the University at Pinar Del Río." He paused to see the reaction on both of their faces, which was excited for my aunt and quite stern and neutral for my uncle. "I also work as a floor manager at a bottling company in downtown Pinar Del Río in order to earn sufficient money to cover my expenses."

Aunt Beatriz had taken a seat beside her husband on the sofa across from us. I was somewhat miffed that Uncle had asked these questions about his occupation, since he already had known from me what Ricardo was presently doing.

"So, you do not live here in Santa Fe, *or even on the Isle of Pines?"* Uncle Pablito asked, as if it was a punishable crime.

Ricardo did not miss a beat, as if he had prepared himself to bear my uncle's scrutiny. "My sister Gladys and I have a house in Santa Fe, and we run a small business there. I am here on the island often and hope to live on it permanently one day soon." The air seemed heavy with a thick tension for reasons I could not fathom.

There was an uncomfortable silence until Aunt Beatriz asked, "Tell us all about your family, Ricardo."

She had known what she was doing. For the next ten minutes, Ricardo described the house he grew up in, the personalities of each of his brothers, sisters, and parents; and then he became even more radiant as he went on to discuss the tobacco farm his papo had worked on throughout his life in Cuba. "I started working with Papo and my brothers on this same tobacco farm when I was nine years old. Papo had instructed us well, and I believe this was because he knew the land and the climate thoroughly."

"You don't want to stay in farming?" Uncle asked.

"I will always love to plant and take good care of things as they grow. In fact, while working to get my BA degree, I had taken a minor academic degree in agriculture."

I was impressed with how well Ricardo was handling himself amid the shenanigans and scrutiny of Uncle Pablito. As well, I was thankful for Aunt Beatriz's pleasantness and support. When their questions had finished, Ricardo offered us a story about a situation he had gotten into with a couple of pigs during his first week working on the farm when he was a child. It was during a heavy rainstorm, and Ricardo and his brothers had been trying to get a family of pigs from a pen which was quickly flooding into a pen on higher ground. Two of the younger pigs had gone astray off the trail between the pens, and his second oldest brother, Leonardo, and he were trying to round them up.

"The raindrops were so large and were coming so hard that they were quite painful as they hit like small missiles on our skin. The two pigs were half-grown and potbellied, squealing like the dickens, as we ran alongside them up a steep hill through the muck of mud and streaming water. Leonardo had just grabbed hold of one of them, and I would not be outdone! I ran quickly farther up the hill and then dove at the hind legs of the other, grabbing each leg, but the pig struggled frantically to get free." He smiled and shook his head. *"But I struggled harder."*

Pausing to take a sip of coconut water, he glanced at me, and I smiled at him. I turned to look across the table, surprised to see Uncle Pablito had folded his newspaper on to his lap and was looking at Ricardo with his full attention. Ricardo then continued.

"I had him with a solid grip, but then, quite suddenly, my small body began sliding downhill along the slickness of the mud and rushing water. *I did not let go of my hold on the animal.* The pig's front legs soon gave out with my downward momentum, and he fell on to his torso. We began accelerating downhill, and I chanced a look only to realize it was *a long hill.* Not wanting to lose him, I pulled the squealing pig close to my body and cradled him against my stomach. Rolling on to my back, I looked, but could find nothing to grasp in order to stop our descent. Gushing water added to our now rapid pace downhill. Finally, through the rain, I saw I was quickly approaching Leonardo, who was standing upright about ten meters away from me with the other young pig in his arms."

Ricardo smiled as he seemed to be remembering this event quite vividly. "Leonardo began backing away from us as we approached, as if he knew what was coming."

I looked at Aunt Beatriz, and she was completely engaged with Ricardo's telling of this story, smiling from ear to ear. I chanced a glance at my uncle, and to my great surprise, his expression was similar.

Ricardo continued. "I stuck out my free arm, and there was no time to think about what I was about to do. As the pig and I passed my brother, I reached out and grabbed Leonardo by his ankle, hoping that by doing so, he could stop our slide. *But just the opposite happened!* As soon as my hand connected to his ankle, Leonardo upended *and fell face first into the mud.* He held on to his pig though, and now both of us, along with our youthful animal charges, were in a free-for-all down the slope, which, by the way, *led all the way to the main estate house!*"

Aunt Beatriz laughed approvingly, and even Uncle Pablito let out a small chuckle despite himself. I laughed and watched Ricardo as he completed the story, something about the owner of the farm coming out and yelling angrily, and that it was not a very good first impression of Ricardo and his talents as a farmhand. Watching him so full of life, I believed I could see into his soulful brown eyes, and what they told me at that moment was that he was going to be a great caretaker for his future wife and children one day. However, more than that, I suddenly had a strong intuitive sense that this man before me would be the best and only man who could ever be my partner in life. The feeling which swept across my soul was that we had known each other for eternity, and now that I had found him once again, *I would never want to be without him along the journey of my life.*

During the brief pause in the conversation following the story of the two pigs, I wondered if my aunt and uncle would give Ricardo and I time together alone with each other. It would not matter, because Ricardo kept their attention by continuing the conversation. He began to discuss his hopes and dreams for the future, informing that he wanted a nice house where he could raise two or three children, with a loving wife who would stay at home to take care of the kids and the house. He said he believed in education and that it was the best way to make great and loyal citizens for our beloved Cuba. When Uncle asked what made him want to become a professor, he informed us that he believed he had such noble aspirations because he had watched his own parents work so hard all their lives, and because they had never had the opportunity to receive an education, this had caused them to remain laborers. "Even in my generation, out of all of my siblings, only my younger sister Manuela and I finished school and graduated successfully."

"Both of your parents are from Spain, originally?" Uncle Pablito asked.

Ricardo nodded. "Yes. My papo is Eduardo Perez-Gomez from Las Palma Islas Canarias, and my mami is Natalia Sanchez Tomas, from Andalusia, Spain."

Aunt Beatriz then asked, "How many brothers and sisters do you have altogether?"

"My parents believed in a large family, as was common for the families from their regions. Within twelve years, they had my oldest sister Gladys, then my oldest brother Paquito, and then Leonardo, Israel, Margarita, Carlos, myself, and the youngest of us all, Manuela. So, altogether, five boys and three girls. I am closest to Gladys, Paquito, Leonardo, and Manuela."

Aunt Beatriz nodded approvingly. "And, how old are you?" she asked.

"I have just turned twenty-seven."

There was a pause once again, and I glanced at Aunt Beatriz, who nodded to me ever so slightly. Ricardo continued to fill every gap which came along.

"In all honesty, we were a poor family," he said. "Since it was so large, we did not often have much extra to go around. We learned to conserve and use everything we had for some good purpose."

"Who was it that owned the farm you all had worked on?" Uncle Pablito asked, as if he might know of them somehow.

"My papo's family had ties all the way back in Las Palma Islas Canarias to the Enrico family, which owned the farm. Both families had a rich heritage of farming back in Spain. The owner's name is Pablo Enrico."

Aunt and Uncle nodded, and then my aunt turned to me and said, "You haven't talked about yourself at all, dear."

And so then, I finally got the chance to talk about my family, the farm, Abuela and Papa Ramon, my cousins, Papo's lumberyard, and my own interests just a bit. The evening sped by quickly. Aunt Beatriz brought out slices of mango and fried plantains for us to snack upon, and Ricardo came up with one story after another to keep us all laughing. Uncle Pablito discussed the store, and how during the summer months they were seeing more and more American tourists.

"They can be a bit obnoxious, to tell you the truth, but they love spending their money on useless things, so I don't mind them at all!"

Ricardo laughed. "I believe you are correct!" Then he did something quite unexpected. Speaking in perfect English, with a thick southern American drawl, he said, "We are Americans, *and what we want, we will buy.* Everything has a price tag on it, *and we will not be wanting for anything!"*

Although we did not understand all that he had said, we got enough of it, and everyone in the room burst out laughing. Aunt Beatriz and Uncle Pablito seemed, like me, to be quite impressed with Ricardo's grasp of English.

"How well do you know English?" Aunt Beatriz asked.

"Fluidly! I took English as my elective courses throughout the four years earning my bachelor's degree at the university. I use it sometimes during a four-hour-long radio show I do every Saturday morning out of Pinar Del Río just in case any Americans may be listening in on it."

"A radio show?" Aunt Beatriz asked.

"Yes. It is produced by the university and called *Agriculture for All!* We try giving tips and important information about the growing season, upcoming climate patterns, soil conditions, new products, and how best to capitalize on the harvest. We play music throughout the show as well."

With that, we began drawing the evening to a close, as it was already going on ten. If there had been any skepticism about the character of my new love interest prior to this visit, I could not imagine that there would be any whatsoever afterwards. For the next three weeks, we met at my aunt and uncle's house each evening at seven, and always, Ricardo was dressed in his finest. By the third outing, of course, I was forced to tell my parents about him. Mami talked with Aunt Beatriz right away, and afterwards, she seemed happy for me. Papo was very concerned at first and took a little bit longer to come around. He talked with Mami and then Uncle Pablito and seemed to feel a little better about it. I promised that one day soon, we would arrange for Ricardo to meet them.

With the summer almost over, Ricardo was due to head back to school and work. The last few weeks had flown by, and I dreaded his departing. He had promised he would write to me every day, and I admit, I knew how men could be once they became busy with their careers, and so part of me doubted that he would. *However, that would not stop me from writing to him since he had given me his address in Pinar Del Río.*

On the day before he was to leave, I was waiting outside our home on the front porch, sipping cool spring water. Cousin Maria Del Carmen had called in the morning, asking if she could meet me at our house, as she had a task I could do for her. I was not sure what it entailed, but since she could find nobody else, I said I would meet with her to discuss it further. Like my sister, Maria Del Carmen had gone into the garment and clothing business. Mostly she would assign other people's unwanted clothing to a store looking to sell it. She would split the profits three ways between the store owner, the person who had assigned her the clothing, and herself. Sure enough, as she had said she would, she came marching over about 1:00 p.m. carrying a large brown bag.

"Hi, cuz!" she said as she climbed the three stairs up the porch. "Thanks for doing this for me. It's rather simple, really, and I would do it myself, but I have to be back at the café to help Mami and Papo."

"I am glad to be of help, Maria, if I am able."

Maria was in her waitress outfit—a black pair of slacks, white button-down shirt, and black bowtie. She put the bag down before me and stooped to show me its contents. Of course, it was clothing—both men's shirts and women's dresses. "These styles are selling quickly, and I have a new outlet for selling them that seems to be quite productive. Two of my best customers informed me—it's a brother and sister who operate a store from their house a bit farther out from our home in Northeast Santa Fe." My heart skipped a beat momentarily as she continued. "They have some money for me from things they sold for me last week, and they are expecting this bag of clothing to put up for sale." She drew a piece of paper from her pocket. "Here's the address. The brother's name is Ricardo, and the sister's is Gladys."

I realized that nobody had spoken to Maria about my dating Ricardo, which I was glad to know. *My cousin had no idea.* I immediately became quite excited as I had not been to Ricardo's house yet, and I had been wanting badly to meet his sister Gladys.

"Would you mind doing this for me?" Maria Del Carmen asked.

I tried showing restraint. *"Of course not."*

"Great! I will pay you for your time, don't worry. I hate to ask, but if you can leave rather soon, that would be great! I told them I would have someone there by two or two-thirty."

"That's fine, Maria, I can leave almost right away. And you do not have to pay me."

Maria nodded with a smile and then turned to head back down the sidewalk. Looking over her shoulder, she said, "Thanks again, Angela! I owe you a favor! I'll come by later this evening when we close to collect the money."

I rushed inside and freshened myself. My hair seemed a little frazzled and curlier than usual due to the humidity and breezes all day, and so I used some of the hairspray I had purchased at the pharmacy the day I had met Ricardo outside by the shoeshine stand.

"Where are you headed off to now?" Mami asked as I made my way to the front door. She had on her kitchen apron, and dusty trails of flour were on it and even a bit in her hair.

I stopped in my tracks and turned to face her. "Mami, *you won't believe this*, but Cousin Maria Del Carmen is in a pinch and needs me to deliver this bag of clothing to one of her new outlets."

"Okay." She looked at me with a puzzled face. "But why then are you so excited, my dear?" she said, wiping her hands on a kitchen towel which was draped over her shoulder.

"*Because of whose business I have to deliver these to*—it is none other than Ricardo and his sister Gladys's house!"

Mami tried acting aloof, but nonetheless a brief smile betrayed her happiness for me. "Okay, well business is business…it usually won't wait, so go—*just be careful!*"

"I will, Mami, I promise." Just then, there was a knock on our front door. *What now?* I took the few steps toward the door and opened it. To my great surprise, my cousin Caruca was standing before me. "Caruca, what a surprise!" I hesitated momentarily, not sure what her visit was about. She, too, was carrying a large paper bag and dressed as stylish as ever, wearing a fashionable light blue women's business suit like the women wore in America. Her hair was tied back in a bun and her face adorned with a moderate amount of just the right makeup. *Beautiful, as always.*

"Angela—I'm glad I caught you! I had been on my way to talk with Maria Del Carmen about selling these high-level shoes at one of her outlets when I ran into her on her way back to the café. She informed me about Ricardo's sister Gladys's store—*I had no idea she was selling so many things there!* Anyway, long story short—I know you are headed that way, and I thought we could go together. I have Josephina holding down the boutique."

"That would be wonderful," I exclaimed.

Mami called to us from the kitchen. "And then when you are through there with business, both of you come home, and I'll have a nice dinner waiting!"

"It's a deal," Caruca shouted.

We began what would be about a twenty-five-minute walk, but the weather had broken finally, and it was a nice warm, not too hot, and *dry* breeze blowing across the island. "I have told no one about you and Ricardo," Caruca said as we made our way down the boulevard heading northeast. "Isn't he on his way back to Pinar Del Río?"

"He is leaving tomorrow first thing. We weren't even certain if he would have the time to get together this evening, and so we had made our goodbyes yesterday evening at your house. You had been working late at the store."

We walked along several more steps, waving hello to a family out in their front yard. As we passed by, Caruca asked, "He still has not met your parents?"

"No, Papo has been too busy at the yard, but we have plans to have him over to the house on his next return trip to the island."

"And when will that be?"

"Just before Christmastime."

For much of the remainder of our walk, Caruca discussed a boy she had met at the beach two weeks prior. He was a teacher at one of the high schools, and she seemed smitten by his great good looks and upbeat personality. "Have you told your parents about him, yet?" I asked her.

"No—*what they don't know can't hurt them.*" She smiled, and I found myself feeling perplexed knowing how stringent Uncle Pablito could be when it came to screening men dating the women he cared about.

We finally arrived. It was a beautiful and large two-story house painted light blue, with a finely landscaped yard. As always, when I knew I might see Ricardo, my heart quickened. *Honestly, though, I did not think it was likely we would see him as he had so many things to accomplish downtown before leaving.* The door was open, and we let ourselves in. Immediately, both Caruca and I admired how they had set up their boutique right in their home. The entire living room and half of the dining room contained several long metal stands full of clothing of all kinds from children's, to men's, to the finest women's styles. Rows of shoes filled shoe racks against the inside wall of the larger room, and wooden bureaus on the opposite wall held more neatly stacked piles of garments. Many vases full of fresh, colorful flowers were scattered among the clothing on shelves and on stands set by themselves, and love songs filled the air.

"Hello, ladies," came a voice from the dining room. We turned, and right away I recognized Ricardo's sister Gladys from a photo of his entire family he had brought to Aunt and Uncle's house last week. Immediately, Gladys flashed a smile of recognition, and I realized Ricardo must have shown her the school photo of me which I had given him. *"Angela?"* she asked.

I nodded. "Gladys, it is so nice to finally meet you!"

She came to me, and we embraced. "For me to meet you, as well!" She stood back a step and took a full gaze at me. "You are every bit as beautiful as your photo, *if not more so in person."*

"You are too kind," I said. I turned to Caruca. "This is my cousin Caruca, Aunt Beatriz and Uncle Pablito's daughter."

Gladys offered her hand, and they shook hands congenially. "This is a quite unexpected, but pleasant surprise." She looked at the bags we both carried. "However, is this about business?"

I explained how we had both come to be at her store this afternoon.

"So Maria Del Carmen is your cousin?"

"Yes, her mami is sister to mine! Here are the new items she wanted you to put up." I handed her the bag. "Also, Maria Del Carman had talked with Caruca about how well your business was doing. She has brought along some high-end shoes that she had hoped to discuss with you the possibility of putting them up in your boutique."

"Certainly, let me take a look." Caruca handed her the bag she had been carrying, and Gladys opened it and started sorting through the shoes. Inspecting several pair closely, she said, "They are wonderful!"

"These might not get top dollar at our store," Caruca said. "Our customers have many stores to choose from near us. I thought perhaps out here where there is not so much competition, they might demand a higher price."

"I think you may be right. They are lovely. My customers would snatch these up in an instant."

Caruca smiled. They engaged in negotiations about fees, and they settled amicably upon a fair share for Gladys, who then went to the register behind the desk at the back of the living room. She took out an envelope of cash and handed it to me. "This is for Maria Del Carmen."

I nodded, and then took the envelope and folded it before placing it in the large pocket of my dress. Gladys then brought us to a table in the dining room. "Come, let me get you something to drink before you make the long walk back home." We took seats at the table, and Gladys disappeared into the kitchen. I could tell Caruca was looking over the entire boutique to decide if she could incorporate any of its ideal presentations for her own store. Soon, Gladys returned with cups of juice and slices of mango on a plate. "Wait, I want to show you something," she said as she scooted down the hallway. I looked at Caruca in bewilderment, and we both wondered what she was going to get.

She returned carrying a large, red leather photo album. Taking the seat between us, Gladys opened it at once. "These are all of our family photos throughout the years!"

I was amazed—most of the photos were in black and white but several of the more current ones were in color. *I could pick out Ricardo in each one.* Even as a baby, he had such an adorable, and even captivating, stare that supplemented his bright smile and perfect facial features. As a boy, he was equally handsome and rugged whether he was at home, on the farm, in school, or playing with his brothers, sisters, and friends. Caruca seemed equally as interested in the photos as I was.

Suddenly, we heard someone coming through the door in the living room. "Hello!" they hollered out. *I knew at once it was Ricardo.* He saw us as he had started heading down the hall and immediately changed direction. I did not know if I should stand to greet him or stay seated, but it did not matter—he came to me right away and put his hands on my shoulders. *"To what do I owe such a pleasant surprise?"* He kissed me on top of my head.

I reached up and gently placed my hands on top of his. Looking up into his beautiful eyes, I explained the nature of our call, and that we were so glad that we could see him once again before he departed. Having already met Caruca on several occasions at Uncle Pablito and Aunt Beatriz's, he greeted her with his warm smile. Looking at his sister, he said, "I will show the ladies all of our wonderful family photos so that I can explain the setting and situation of each of them!"

"Go right ahead!" Gladys said, standing to allow Ricardo to have her seat. Just then, some customers entered the store, and she excused herself to attend to their needs.

Ricardo sat and began going over each of the first few pages of photos, explaining who everyone was, and then also *where they were, or what they had been engaged in doing.* I could tell how proud he was of each of the people in the photos. His parents were always standing beside each other and usually holding hands, and it seemed they had been very close. "This was the day of the pig affair," he said showing us a photo of him and his brother Leonardo, covered from head to toe in mud. "We had just come home and Mami went at once to fetch the camera."

As time drew on, I began to dread that I would have another opportunity to say goodbye to Ricardo. I was never one who was very comfortable with goodbyes, and soon both he and Caruca sensed my sudden change in mood.

"What is wrong, darling?"

With that, tears began to form in my eyes. Caruca got up and came behind me to pat me on the shoulder. "Now, my dear, what is it?"

Tears now flowing down my cheeks, I said, "Oh—this is all just so marvelous, and to think that it will be all ending is horrendous!"

Ricardo scooted closer to me and wrapped his arm around my shoulders. "My love," he said in his confident and calm voice. "But this is not an ending at all. In fact, *it is just the opposite.* This is just the beginning!" He took out a handkerchief from the front pocket of his suit coat, and he dabbed my eyes and nose.

I suddenly felt so silly and could not think of what to do or say next.

Ricardo continued, "If I did not have to return to Pinar Del Río in order to fulfill both my work and study obligations there, you would see I would stay here, and we would be together each and every day." Gently placing his index finger beneath my chin, he lifted my head, which had been bent down to the ground. Our eyes met once again, and I searched them for any evidence which would support or deny my fears. "My darling, you will soon see that I will call you almost each and every day, and I will send you many letters and cards." He tenderly stroked my cheek with his thumb. "I promise, Angela, *this is not over by any means.*"

I turned and brushed my eyes with the back of my hand. I then looked deeply into Ricardo's joy-filled eyes before turning and looking behind me at Caruca, who had a thin smile on her face as she looked at me with concern. She gave me a slight nod and with it, tried to confirm what I had been wanting to believe with all my heart and soul: that I could trust Ricardo's words—*that he truly loved me and was planning on making his life together with me for all time.* I looked back at Ricardo and despite myself, I smiled at him.

"My love, where else could I possibly meet as fine a woman as you?" Ricardo said to me. I looked at his watch and then suddenly stood, as it was time to go. We slowly walked to the door and saw that Gladys was finishing her sale to two customers. It looked to me, in my brief glance at the counter, that two pairs of Caruca's shoes and three dresses from Maria Del Carmen were among the items being packaged. We nodded hello to the two happy customers as they passed us by on the way out, and then Gladys made her way over to us.

Ricardo said, "Such beautiful and refined black curls in your long, flowing hair. And such a beautiful yellow dress—*Angela, my dear, you have my entire heart for all time!"* Each of us embraced and said farewell, and for Gladys, we added that we would see her very soon.

Walking home, Caruca and I were mostly quiet. For me, the second goodbye to Ricardo was as harsh as the first one had been, but perhaps I had more faith that this would not be the end.

"He truly loves you," Caruca said when we were about halfway home.

No matter how I tried, Uncle Pablito's words about Ricardo being a womanizer kept on returning to my mind to haunt me. I suppose it could also be that I had heard many stories about men and the dastardly things they would do to get what they wanted from a woman. "I do not think so," I replied.

"Oh, Angela—stop that! *How can you say that after all he has done to be with you so often during the past three weeks?"*

I looked up at a mother of two babies in a stroller as they walked by us. "I don't know, Caruca. *Do you truly believe he will come back to me?"*

"Yes, I do."

I determined to allow Caruca's wisdom to overcome my own anxiety for the remainder of the walk home. As we finally approached the house, *I knew right away that something was wrong.* Antonio and Fernando were out front with Mami, and each of them were looking somewhat frantically in a different direction. As we started up the driveway, Antonio had gotten into one of the delivery trucks from the lumberyard and was backing out very quickly. Fernando ran over to us. "You haven't seen Papo's red delivery truck going by, have you?"

"No," I answered. *"What's the matter, Fernando?"*

He shook his head. "It seems Estrella borrowed the keys to the red truck as soon as I got home from the yard. *She and Luis just took off for a joyride!"*

My eyes opened wide in frustration. "That Estrella!" She had just turned thirteen and for months had been professing to anybody who would listen that she believed the age to get your driver's license should be thirteen, not sixteen. Of course, wanting a chance for a fun time, it would take nothing to convince Luis to go along with her.

"What can we do?" Caruca asked.

"Papo is already out searching in the tan truck, and now Antonio has gone hunting for them. Hopefully, one of them will find them soon," Fernando said.

"How well can she drive?" Caruca asked.

"Oh, pretty darn well for a thirteen-year-old girl," Fernando answered, smiling.

Suddenly, we heard Mami hollering at us from the porch. "C'mon! *Let's eat before dinner gets cold."*

With those orders, we came inside and washed up. Sitting at the table, I gave the blessing, adding a special intention that Estrella and Luis be safe and return home in one piece. We ate in silence at first, since the food was as good as always, and would snatch all one's attention. Mami had made Cuban beef picadillo with fresh tomatoes, onions, olives, red peppers, and whole-leaf cilantro over white rice. However, after only a few forkfuls, Mami could not help herself.

"How is your Ricardo doing?"

"Mami, his sister Gladys is just wonderful. Her boutique is amazing. Ricardo returned home as we were looking through photos of him and his family from years ago."

Mami nodded.

"I think you will like Ricardo and his family when you finally get to meet, Aunt Catalina," Caruca said. *"Ricardo is a real gentleman."*

Mami smiled and nodded, and then suddenly we heard the front door opening. Luis came waltzing in, dancing along to a song he was making up, singing out loud to himself or perhaps for all to hear. *"We are the best drivers in the world... We can drive you anywhere, come with us! It's Luis and Estrella's taxi service, opened just for you!"*

Mami dropped her fork loudly onto her plate.

Before Mami could say anything, immediately we heard Papo's voice calling behind Luis. *"Get to your room at once—no singing and no dancing!"*

Next, we saw Estrella being led into the house by Papo's firm grip, with Antonio only a step or two behind them. Papo stopped in the hallway and looked in at us. "You wouldn't believe it! They had gotten all the way to the church!"

Mami shook her head.

Estrella smiled and said, *"I thought you would be happy with us!* We went to say devotionals to the Blessed Mother!"

With that, Caruca could not contain herself any longer, and she burst out laughing. Fernando then joined her as I tried desperately to hide my smile in my napkin.

Papo said, leading Estrella down the hall, "C'mon—off to your room with you!"

Antonio joined us at the table. "*What a pair those two make!*" He began filling his plate with the picadillo. "This looks and smells wonderful, Mami. Should we make two plates for them?"

I watched Mami closely. "Not yet. Let them think about it first, and then I will bring them their dinner once they are not sure whether or not they will even get any!"

Antonio nodded as Papo sat down at the head of the table. *"Now we have to make another trip back to the church after dinner.* We had to leave the truck they drove there for now."

I took it as a good sign that our family had one date planned for church that had been previously unexpected!

Chapter Five

It was going to be a long four months. However, *I was happy*—as he had promised, by October, Ricardo was calling almost every day, and because he had departed for Pinar Del Río only days before my birthday, he had made up for it by sending me in the mail a beautiful silver bracelet with two pearl hearts attached. One had been engraved with *Angela* and the other, *Ricardo*.

Mami and I had started listening to his radio show on Saturday mornings now that we knew where to find it on the dial. He always sounded professional and engaged the audience with plenty of amusing and informative stories. For the very first one we had tuned in, Ricardo had been talking with a cohost for the week about the best ways to get rid of pests in the soil and on plants. I was amazed at his sophisticated knowledge and his command of the subject. He had promised to play some music after a commercial break, and it shocked Mami and I when he came back on the air and said, *"I would like to dedicate this next song to my one true love—the finest of ladies a guy could ever hope to know!"* I was in utter shock! I turned to Mami with an expression of absolute surprise and accompanied by a huge smile. *"Angela, my darling, this one is for you all the way across the waters to the Isle of Pines! I love you, my dear, and can't wait to hold you in my arms once again!"*

Mami returned my smile with her own and with an equally surprised look on her face. She then reached out and pinched me on the cheek, which I was glad she did, because at that point, I was certain I had been dreaming! Ricardo mentioned me several more times that day, and almost every week, he would devote at least three endearing love songs to me!

I had been back to see Gladys on occasion, and she had even prepared two dinners for her and I. Caruca and Maria Del Carmen were doing a good amount of business with her, but we had decided not to let Maria know about Ricardo and I just yet, as she tended to be a talker and I did not want undue attention. Pilar had returned from Bejucal, and it was good finally seeing her once again. She had become a lovely woman, but thankfully, she still maintained her playful nature. I kept on looking for a good time to tell her about Ricardo, but I had wanted to spend time with her again before I did. Carmen, Pilar, and I soon became inseparable, and we often went out to the café together, down to the lake, and then there were our quite frivolous shopping expeditions into town. We began helping collect clothes from friends and neighbors to distribute to both Caruca and Maria Del Carmen, and I was still assisting Mami and Lilliana with sewing new clothes while helping to mend the ones for my cousins that we took on consignment, as needed.

I could not wait for December to arrive. Of course, because of Christmas, but this year I would be getting an extra-special Christmas gift. *Ricardo was due to visit on December 21, and he would have almost the entire week to stay in Isle of Pines.* As the date approached, I became a little nervous, as our first obligation would be having lunch at our house when Ricardo would finally meet my family. He would be arriving back to Santa Fe by bus late in the afternoon on Saturday, the twenty-first, and he and I would get together that evening at his house. Lunch with my family at my house was to be after church the next day.

Our phone conversations were grand but somehow only made me want to be with him all the more. He would talk about his courses and the people he worked with at the bottling plant, and I would discuss my family and daily activities. We were on the phone a week before he was due to arrive, and I was sitting in our living room all by myself, thankfully, as Mami had Lilliana and Estrella shopping in town, and since it was early afternoon, everyone else was working. Only Luis was home, and he seemed to be keeping himself busy running around the yard with some of his toys.

Ricardo's voice was soothing and had the effect of calming me. I pulled my legs up on the Queen Anne chair and listened to him intently. *"My dear, can you wait until next week? I cannot! Seeing your lovely smile and that beautiful face will be the highlight of my past four months!"*

I blushed and was glad nobody was around to see me. "Oh, Ricardo, *I cannot wait!* My days seem to go on endlessly without purpose. My heart longs for you like I never knew a heart could do!"

"Patience, my love. And I have a surprise which can hardly wait even another day, let alone seven more. Let me have your address so I can come to see you as soon as I get off the bus in Santa Fe." We were both silent for a moment, and then Ricardo continued. *"Angela, my love, I want to ask you something in person, but fear I cannot put if off any longer and might just ask over the telephone!"*

I suddenly had the feeling I knew what he wanted to do—*ask if I would be his steady girl*, but I knew I had to be insistent. It was not right that I give him an answer without him having met my family first! *Because of my devotion to Mami and Papo, and knowing their expectations so well, it would be the only fair and just thing to do.* "Wait, my love. I think I know your intentions, but I must insist—Papo and Mami have to meet you first and must be given the chance to give us their blessing." He was silent, and so I continued. "As for my address, you already know the house! It is the first white house adjacent to the farm where the bus stops!"

Finally, Ricardo spoke again. *"All this time, I had no idea! Okay, I will speak with your papo right after our lunch at your house on Sunday. And now, I have a great idea! Wave to me from your porch on Saturday when you see me getting off of the bus! I should be arriving around 4:30!"*

"I cannot wait! These days will pass much too slowly until I see you once again, darling. Please take care and travel safely." I ran through my mind the impending get-together. "And one last thing, my love, when Papo asks you questions, *do not hesitate at all in giving your response.* I know he is going to love you as much as I do—and that goes for Mami and my entire family as well!"

When I had hung up, suddenly I heard Luis's squeaky voice from behind me. "How is that handsome boyfriend of yours doing, sis?"

I turned and knew at once he had been listening in on my conversation. "Luis!" I got up and ran after him and wound up chasing him throughout the yard until I caught him and pinned him to the ground. Tickling him beneath his armpits, he giggled incessantly as I demanded, *"Don't ever do that again!"*

Somehow, I made it through until Saturday. I could not wait to see my Ricardo getting off the bus, knowing we would just wave to each other for now, but that I would be in his arms this evening. *Wouldn't you know it?* Cousin Maria Del Carmen came for an unexpected visit late in the afternoon, just as I was preparing to sit on the porch and wait to see the bus coming from downtown.

"I am taking a break from work," she said, "and I knew just the right spot to do so—*on your front porch!"* It surprised me that she was wearing a light red dress and not her waitress uniform, and that she had fixed her hair and had put on mascara and lipstick.

I invited her to sit on the swinging chair, and then I went into the kitchen to prepare two glasses of chilled lemonade, which I brought out and gave one of them to Maria before sitting down beside her. It was a mild afternoon with high puffy clouds scooting gently across the blue sky and with a perfect light breeze.

"I must tell you, Angela," Maria said after sipping her drink. "I have an ulterior motive for having come today." I looked at her quizzically. "My friend Leddy came rushing into the café just a short time ago, telling me she had been at the pharmacy when she saw *the most perfect man scouring the shelves.* He was tall, handsome…a real gentleman—and Leddy overheard him tell the clerk that he was buying things to bring home to his sister and someone else, possibly an aunt of his. The clerk happened to ask where did his sister live, and when he responded, Leddy realized it was only several blocks away from here!" Maria patted her hair and smiled. "She said that as he was leaving the pharmacy, he mentioned to the clerk that he had a few more stores to visit, and that he would then be taking the bus and getting off right here at the corner, where for some reason, *he was expecting to see a beautiful woman!"*

I could not believe it! It must have been Ricardo! I tried acting indifferent, and I looked at Maria as if I could care less. "And you think you might get his attention somehow?"

She nodded. "Let's face it, Angela. Neither of us are getting any younger, and finding a good man these days is not easy by any means." She glanced up the avenue in search of movement. "*Yes,* since he is obviously interested in meeting a beautiful girl, I believe if he acts at all interested in me when he sees us waving at him, that I might just go and strike up a conversation with him. *You might consider doing as such yourself, depending upon which of us he looks at more closely!"*

I turned away from Maria and allowed myself a brief smile. When I was about to turn back to say something, we suddenly heard the bus bouncing along the road, and soon enough, we could see it coming our way. Maria sat up straight and smoothed her dress, then carefully ran her fingers through her long brown hair once again. She was gazing at the bus intently, and I realized this situation could get quite awkward. I watched as the bus came to a stop not a hundred meters away in front of our house.

We waited apprehensively, and then a moment later, we watched him climbing down the exit stairs. He was the only one to get off the bus, and he was wearing a long-sleeved, light blue shirt with the sleeves rolled up, and carrying three large bags. As soon as he hit the ground, he looked up at the porch, and seeing both of us, he seemed confused for just an instant before he flashed his gorgeous bright smile in our direction. Continuing to glance our way with his handsome good looks, he then put down the package that was in his right hand and waved toward us, shouting, *"Good afternoon, ladies!"*

Maria was gushing excitement and waving back at him frantically, and for a moment, I feared Ricardo might believe he should come up our driveway to say hello. As she continued waving at him, Maria shouted, hopefully, *"Good afternoon!"*

I tried to smile and wave tentatively, but more than that, I was attempting to give Ricardo the message to hurry along to his sister.

For an instant, I saw him look questioningly at me, and I gave a short and contrite shake of my head. Ricardo understood, and he nodded politely, then picked up the bag he had put to the ground, turned, and began walking down the cross avenue.

I quickly faced Maria, saying, *"Well, he does not seem that interested in either of us, that's for sure!"* I had also made a list of back-up reasons in my head as to why she should not pursue him.

Looking at me with unbridled excitement, and not to be discouraged, Maria said, *"Angela*—did you see the way he looked at me?" Knowing he had been looking at me, I chuckled to myself, but otherwise was not sure how to respond to my cousin and so I remained silent at first. *"I felt his eyes burning a hole through me!"* She continued.

Just when I thought for certain she was about to get on her feet and go after him, I said, "Now that he's in town, I bet it won't be long until he winds up at the café, and you'll probably be there and get to serve him." *I must remember to warn Ricardo to stay away from the café for now.* Thankful when Maria stayed in the swing chair beside me, I sipped my drink and added, "He sure was handsome, though, and I can certainly see why Leddy told you about him."

"I am determined to find out who he is and where that sister of his lives!" Maria said, and soon departed back to the café as she had to be there before the dinner rush began.

That evening, after dinner, I dressed in my light-blue dress and looked after each detail of my appearance. Once sufficiently satisfied, I told Mami and Papo that I had to run to Gladys's to pick up some money for Caruca and that I would stay to visit with Gladys and Ricardo for just a bit since Ricardo had just returned home.

"Be home by nine," Papo said as I left the house.

I could not walk quickly enough, and I felt as if my feet were tripping over each other as I made my way. When I got there, the house was lit with three lamps lined along the front walk, even though it was not quite dusk. I walked up to the front door excitedly, but before I could knock, *the door swung open, and Ricardo was before me with a smile and open arms.* I immediately fell into them and rested my head on his chest as he held me silently for many moments. Time stood still and nothing else mattered, and I do not even know how many minutes passed until he ushered me into the house. Gladys was waiting in the dining room with some snacks and drinks. Once we settled and sat, Ricardo asked, *"Who was that sitting beside you earlier on the porch?"*

I rolled my eyes. "My cousin, Maria Del Carmen! Gladys knows her from business." I explained what her friend Leddy had overheard, and that she had rushed to tell Maria about coming to meet him at the bus stop.

Ricardo and Gladys burst out in laughter. "I think I have a gentleman in mind that might be perfect for Maria," Gladys said. "He is a good friend of mine, and his name is Alberto Rodriguez. In fact, he owns the hardware store a few doors down from Maria's family's café. Although, come to think of it, *we must keep this from our youngest sister, Manuela, as she has had a growing crush on Alberto these past several months and wants to go and see him every time she comes to visit with me from Pinar Del Río."*

We began to catch up with each other, and then Ricardo suddenly brought out a small package wrapped in red paper and with a large maroon bow. I searched his eyes as he said, "Go on, open it now, *don't worry."*

I took it from his hands and carefully untied the bow, and then gently loosened the tape holding the wrapping paper. It was a blue cardboard box, and I became quite intrigued and a bit apprehensive. Ricardo and Gladys were both smiling as I struggled to lift the top off the box. Finally doing so, I took a deep breath and revealed a beautiful set of gold earrings in the shape of a rose, each with a small red ruby inset. Tears came to my eyes because they were so beautiful and perfect. *I looked up at Ricardo and tried smiling.* He reached over and gently kissed me on the lips as he said, "*For my beautiful Angela.* Gold and roses are not enough, but they are a start."

I had to wind up rushing home because I had stayed a little later than I had planned, and it was close to nine. *Also, I could not wait to show Mami, Josephine, and Lilliana my earrings.* When they saw them, they were absolutely thrilled on my behalf.

Josephina eventually said, “My boyfriend is taking rather long getting to the next level of commitment in our relationship. I am glad to see some men do not hesitate!”

Mami added, “Each man follows his own timeline, do not fret. *However, if you think he is taking too long, then you must let him know you will not wait forever!*”

Morning came quickly, and as usual, church was very crowded. I could hardly focus on any of the readings or even Padre Jorge’s sermon this Sunday, and I rushed home immediately afterwards to get ready for our lunch engagement. Abuela and Papa Ramon would be coming, and Mami and I had so much to get ready. As we got busy, out of the corner of my eyes, I watched Papo to see how he was preparing for Ricardo’s visit. He gave nothing away at first; however, as time drew near, I saw that he went out of his way to carefully fold and arrange the week’s newspapers on the stand beside his favorite chair in the living room. Ordinarily, he would leave them haphazardly in a pile in no particular order.

We began setting the table and bringing out some of the side dishes and appetizers when Abuela and Papa Ramon arrived. Papa Ramon greeted me with a smile and hug, and then he went to sit with Papo in the living room. Abuela had brought several dishes along, and she fell right in to help us finish setting the main table. She then prepared a small table in the kitchen for my younger siblings. I was looking over the main table a few minutes later when I saw a blue Chevy coming up our driveway. Papo must have seen it, as well, because he suddenly stood and looked out the dining room window. *Whose car was it?* I hoped it might be Ricardo, and sure enough, a moment later, after parking the car, *my love got out of it.* Papo glanced at me with a stern expression, informing me to stay out of his business for now. He marched out the front door and met Ricardo out by the blue Chevy. I watched as my Papo and my love engaged in rapid conversation and tried to remember to breathe as the minutes passed along. They were each quite animated, but otherwise, I could not hear a word of it.

At some point, Mami came and stood behind me, watching them for a moment or two. I took a little comfort when I realized that Ricardo was smiling as often as he could, and that Papo seemed relaxed for the most part. When she could not stand it any longer, Mami said, "Wait here," and she went out and joined them.

"Don't worry, my pumpkin," Papa Ramon said from his chair. "These are all the things a good father does to make sure his loving daughter is going to be well cared for. *It's only a little painful,* and it will soon pass, you will see."

Abuela then called to us unexpectedly from the dining room. *"My papo frightened Papa Ramon so much that he did not call or come visit me for three days after!"*

They both burst out in laughter. When I turned to look back at Ricardo and my parents, finally, it was done. They had broken up their encounter, and I watched intently to make sure Ricardo was heading toward the front door of our house and not back to his car. *He was following Mami and Papo!* When he came in, I immediately embraced him and then took him around the house, introducing him to all of my siblings and to my grandparents. Soon enough, we were sitting at the table, and Papo and Ricardo carried on for many more minutes about politics and baseball. *They both liked the New York Yankees, which to me was a good sign.* When he could, Papa Ramon engaged my darling with talk about the weather for the winter and how it might affect the crops come springtime. I said the blessing, and then we passed around the plates to fill our dishes. Scooping some rice and beans into my plate, I realized that it felt like Ricardo was, *and had always been,* a part of our family. Relief flooded through me as I found myself smiling, while listening to their inspirited discussions. Mami glanced at me at one point and gave me her full smile of approval. Abuela did not need to say a word, and I knew that she was as happy as could be.

Later that evening, after cleaning up, and as the rest of my family returned to their normal Sunday evening activities, Ricardo and I sat on the swinging chair on the front porch, sipping cocktails of rum and coconut milk. He knew I had been dying to hear what Papo and he had discussed when he had first arrived earlier.

"Basically, the entire crux of the conversation was my assuring your papo, and then your mami, *that I was an honorable man and that my intentions were true."* He looked at me with a smile and then took hold of my hand. "They wanted to know if I would be in a position to take good care of you once I am to finish with my doctoral program. *I assured them I would be.* They asked if I could promise that I would be moving out here to the island permanently, and I told them that I could not do that because I was not certain a suitable position for me would become available here."

I nodded. We had discussed this issue minimally over the past year or so, and I knew how difficult it would be for Ricardo to be promised the position and the money he had been already making in Pinar Del Río.

"Everything went fine, Angela. Truly it did." I was a bit relieved to hear him say that, and I squeezed his hand, but I wanted to know his opinion about my family, for I had hoped he had taken fondly to them all. *Should I ask directly?* In my silence, Ricardo suddenly grew concerned, and he asked, *"What is it, my dear?* Please tell me—you seem distracted or worried somehow."

I took a deep breath of air, letting it out in a long and slow plume. "Well, I suppose I just want to know…" I was fearful, somehow thinking that my abrupt question would be too much for Ricardo to answer so soon after having met them.

"What, darling? Please tell me."

"All right. I wondered if you could tell me, truthfully, *what did you think of my family and did you like them?"*

He seemed relieved to discover that was all I was concerned about.

"Like them? *I loved your family!* Every one of them—from Papa Ramon and Abuela, to Josephina and Estrella. From your papo and mami, to Lilliana, Antonio, *but especially Fernando and Luis!* Listen, darling—families like yours do not come along too often. *They were great*—so close to each other, so humorous and lively. I know people well enough—you've got a great family…"

And with that, I believed Ricardo's sentiments, and I felt closer to him than I had before. I smiled and then suddenly his expression became intense. I searched his eyes, unsure what was next. He smiled and placed his free hand on top of both of our clasped hands.

Looking at me with the sincerest eyes I had ever seen on any man, he said, "Angela, my love…my one true light and hope, *will you be my one and only true and steady girlfriend, and take me as your one and only true and steady boyfriend?"*

I was relieved and filled with gratitude, love for Ricardo, and joy for our bright future. I returned his intense gaze and smiled with a face full of love. "*I do*…I mean, *I will,"* I said, realizing my slight slip and hoping it did not throw him off. He kissed me beneath the porch canopy, and I felt like I never wanted to remove my lips from him ever again.

We had a fantastic Christmas Eve celebration at our house, and both Gladys and Ricardo were with us the entire day and all the way through Christmas Eve Mass. Gladys was a hit with Mami and Abuela and worked as hard as the rest of us in the meal preparation, serving, and then cleaning up. Ricardo took the boys out to the field in the backyard, and they had a game of baseball which lasted all the way to sunset. Gladys, Mami, Lilliana, Josephina, and I relaxed out back after the meal, watching the boys' game, and as Gladys began discussing her boutique, talking about pointers of the business, Lilliana and Josephina turned the discussion toward the types of women's clothing which were most popular nowadays. Gladys loved Lilliana's work and had seen her dresses demand top prices with her customers. We all cleaned up, dressed, and got ready for mass, and during the fully attended service, Padre Jorge recounted our Christmas blessings. I was happy to see Ricardo enjoying his sermon, and soon enough, mass *along with the entire evening* were drawing to a close.

The Thursday prior to Ricardo's departure, I had planned on a picnic at a small lake amid the green fields which ran for acres across the avenue from our house. I had insisted that all of my close cousins, and my friend Pilar, take off from work or whatever else they had planned, in order to join Ricardo and I; however, I had not told them at first about Ricardo joining us. The night before, Mami and I had made sandwiches and packed drinks and necessities into the picnic basket.

As we started down the trail, Pilar began discussing opening a boutique of her own and Carmen, Maria, and Caruca gave her some details about the business. It was decided that she would work for Maria and Caruca at first to get a better idea of business practices. Finally, uncertain why today's event was so important, Maria Del Carmen asked me, *"Angela, just what is this all about?"*

I had it all planned out how I was going to tell them. Of course, Caruca already knew, but at my request, she acted as if she did not. Ricardo had planned on meeting us at our chosen picnic spot in half an hour. I looked back at Maria, *"Well, I was not sure how I was going to tell everyone the news and this seemed like the best way."* I was leading the way, and as I heard the birds singing happily within the forest on either side of the trail, I felt my confidence rising. *"Girls—I have been dating a man for the past five months.* I did not tell everyone because I was not sure if it would even last."

At first, they were silent, and I realized that nobody knew how to respond or what to say. Finally, Carmen said, *"Well, that's a relief. I was beginning to wonder about you."*

The girls laughed, and then her sister Maria added, "Why have you kept it such a secret? *We all date now,* and then we live to tell all about it!"

Caruca cut her off. "How serious of a love interest is he, Angela?"

Having arrived at our spot—a pristine clearing with a pine needle bed and perfect view of the blue waters of the lake—we put our bundles down, and Caruca began helping me lay out our blankets. I answered her as I smoothed the first blanket across the ground. "He is as fine a gentleman as a girl could hope to meet. I would say he is very intent on me, and he has already met my family."

Not one to be taken off guard, Pilar turned toward me. *"Angela—you're so young!* Are you sure you want to be tied down to just one man already?"

"This one, *yes, I do.*" I paused, opened one of the baskets, and began taking some items out. Stopping, I looked up at each of the women present. "You shall see for yourselves, as he is destined to join us here in about ten minutes."

All the girls looked at one another in shock. There was silence as we went about setting everything out. I glanced at Caruca, who restored my confidence by giving me a quick nod and smile. We took our places on the blanket and Maria Del Carmen poured coconut water into cups for each of us. "Maybe he has a brother," she said.

I looked at her and knew the moment had come, since I did not want her to be caught off guard. I sipped my water, put my cup down beside me, and said, *"In fact, Maria, you already saw him."*

She turned to me, aghast. "*What do you mean, Angela?* Do I know him? Is he a customer?"

I smiled. "No—nothing like that. Last week, on my porch. Remember the man getting off the bus that your friend Leddy had told you about?"

Her eyes opened wide. *"Angela, it can't be!"*

I nodded enthusiastically. "His name is Ricardo Gomez, and his sister you already know quite well—*Gladys Gomez!"*

"Oh my God!" Maria burst out.

Suddenly, we all turned when we heard a man's voice calling out, *"Did I just hear my name?"* Ricardo surprised us as he came off the trail, heading right toward us. He looked as stunning as ever, with his hair perfectly styled and wearing tan pants and his blue guayabera. The ladies all got to their feet, and I made introductions. Maria seemed humble, if not a bit embarrassed; but otherwise, *Ricardo was well-received.* We had a fine lunch as my darling used his skills at storytelling to keep them all entertained with his wonderful adventures. It was a nice and relaxing affair, and I was glad my best friend and cousins were developing a positive feeling for the man that I loved.

Ricardo left for Pinar Del Río the next morning and would call and write me letters almost daily for the next four years. The year following meeting my family, the radio station hired him to do their daily *Agricultura Para Todos* morning show, and he was so busy between that, finishing his doctoral program, and working full-time at the bottling company that he was only able to return to Isle of Pines one time over the following four years. To make up for his lack of ability to get together, he had begun to write me poetic verses, which he would then read over the radio. *They were all about me—my*

eyes, my smile, my concern for others and my family, and they melted my heart each day when I heard a new one.

Every birthday, I received a ring from him in the mail, and for the holidays, cards which made me smile and sometimes laugh. Other gifts and flowers also came to me quite often and unexpectedly. *Each time he tried planning a group of days to take off in order to visit, something else came up, and he had to cancel his trip.* It was frustrating, nonetheless. Josephina was first to get married, and then, believe it or not, Antonio. Lilliana, and then even Fernando, began dating new partners seriously. I sometimes wondered if I was waiting in vain, and if we would truly ever get married. *Ricardo and I talked about this, and then finally, he did something about it.*

We were on the phone with each other on a Saturday night in the dead of winter. We had come to a stall in our conversation, when he said, "I think it is best if we marry, Angela." *He had just proposed to me over the phone. It was February of 1950.*

I agreed at once. He bought an engagement ring and mailed it to me. My cousins looked at me doubtfully, but I knew in my heart his proposal was sincere and true. A week after his proposal, Ricardo said, "Because of my jobs and finishing my degree, I cannot take much time off. *However, let us set the date for marriage to be December 27 of this year.* I will come to your house on December 24. My Uncle Adrian is a friend of the notary, and we can have the ceremony at my house on the island—Gladys will do all of the planning and make the arrangements. The two of you can discuss all your preferences."

I was at once ecstatic!

Ricardo finished his doctorate degree in pedagogy in early December of that year.

Prior to the date of his planned arrival, it was three days of running around to get ready. Lilliana had made me a gorgeous white wedding gown, and we had collected flowers from all the nearby woods and gardens. I suppose I was getting cold feet the closer we got to the day—and I was not even certain if he would come for the wedding. On December 24, Papo planned to roast a pig, and all my relatives would be over for the celebration of Jesus's birth. Earlier that afternoon, I showered and dressed up in my finest garments for the feast. *Mami and Abuela knew how uncertain I felt. I kept as busy as I could with helping them set tables, fill serving dishes, and that morning, I had even made the dough for my now famous tortas, which I fried right before the guests began to arrive.* Of course, everyone present had also already been invited to my wedding, and I felt like all eyes were watching me the entire evening. *The later it got without Ricardo's appearance, the more I felt like we were all in for a big disappointment.* Like me, they had expected Ricardo's presence earlier in the evening.

By eight o'clock, the butterflies which had been flittering in my stomach all day long now felt more like a herd of cattle. *I became beside myself with worry that Ricardo would not show,* and at one point, Papa Ramon had to take me aside.

He said to me, "*You are a beautiful woman, and he is a fool if he has chosen to go against his word.* I believe in my heart he will be here soon. It's Christmastime, and the ferry to the island is probably not on any regular schedule." He smiled at me and then gave me a hug. I felt a little better perhaps, *but not so much better.*

One of the neighbor's children began setting off fireworks out in our front yard, and we all went to watch. Under the dazzling display of magenta sparks, suddenly a car came down the avenue and slowed as it approached our driveway. It then stopped in front of the house, behind the line of other automobiles parked there already. I wondered who it was and peered intensely at the automobile, though it was very dark, and it was difficult at first to see. With the next bright explosion of white light from a showering rocket, I was able to see the car was a blue Chevy. *Could it be Gladys's automobile?* When the passenger stepped out, *I knew at once it was Ricardo!* Gladys got out of the driver's seat and another man came from the back seat.

The entire gathering became silent, and all eyes turned to me as the three new arrivals made their way to our front yard. I then realized that the man from the back seat was Ricardo's Uncle Adrian, *the one who knew the notary who would be performing our service.* Trembling as Ricardo approached me at a brisk pace, he soon smiled and waved his arm in a grand fashion, welcoming everyone's attention. He then immediately fell on to his right knee and took my hand into his. *"Angela, my love, will you be so kind as to marry me?"*

I had to catch my breath and was soon fighting tears as I lifted him back to his feet and embraced him with all my might. *"Yes, yes, and again yes!" I said, loud enough for all to hear!*

It was a picture-perfect day—bright blue skies, a brisk northerly wind which cooled us, and not a cloud to dampen our spirits. The house and yard were packed with dozens of beautiful golden vases filled with flowers of all kinds and colors. All the chairs were covered with rose-colored cloth, as were the tables. A gazebo shrouded with white roses arched over the platform where the ceremony would be performed.

It seemed like the entire town had come for our wedding. I tried to take it all in, but it felt more like a dream and I still could not believe how perfect everything was. Papo marched me down the aisle, with Estrella as flower girl before us. Antonio manned the phonograph, and he played all the right tunes. Mami and Abuela looked so proud, honored, and joy-filled at the front of the procession as did Papa Ramon. However, it was Ricardo who stole the show. As handsome as ever and very dignified, his brother Leonardo had flown in and was his best man. Gladys and all my siblings, besides Antonio, were in the first row, while my cousins and Pilar filled the second. Everyone was dressed in their finest gowns and suits. We had written our own vows and had learned them by heart. They were said with full confidence, on both our parts, that they would be fulfilled to the highest degree.

That same day after a robust reception, we took an airplane, my first time ever, into Havana. I was so happy, and I did not believe it was possible for anybody to be happier. I had changed from my white wedding gown, which Mami would keep for me for now, and I was wearing a green jacket which Aunt Lucia had made for me, a rose-colored dress made by my sister Lilliana, along with a black hat given as a present by Luis. Our destination was the Hotel Ritz, which was known as the finest hotel in all of Havana. It was spectacular in its design and accommodations, and we could not have asked for, or expected, anything more.

Ricardo and I called for room service that evening and for the entire next day.

On Friday, we ventured out to see the sites—huge buildings all around us constructed in glorious Spanish architecture amid a bustling metropolis with casinos, fine waterfront restaurants, museums, zoos, *and you name it!* We tried to do a little bit of everything, but that turned out to be impossible, and so we settled on enjoying walking about and visiting the stores down by the seaport. I was mesmerized by watching so many people from every country imaginable with all their funny accents. I loved the Americans, especially, with their casual tropical clothes and informal attitudes.

On Saturday, believe it or not, *we had another wedding to attend.* This one was for Ricardo's cousin, who lived here in the city. The main importance to me was that I would finally get to meet Ricardo's Mami and some of his other relatives. Ricardo's Papo had passed away years before, and because he was not comfortable talking about it, I had not learned this until last year. Now that I knew, Ricardo would discuss his papo's life with me frequently, and whenever he did, he always mentioned how close his parents had been.

After having taken a bus out to their neighborhood in the southwest part of Havana, we began walking and looking for the cousin's house. Although we had the address, the problem was that the houses were not numbered consistently. As Ricardo was looking to our right, I glanced across the street to our left, *and I immediately saw his Mami in front of a house looking up the street in the opposite direction from our approach.* I had recognized her instantly from a framed photo Gladys had on the wall in the entrance hall of their home, and which I had looked at often when visiting. I grabbed Ricardo by the arm and pointed with my free hand. *"Look, isn't that Mami?"*

Ricardo smiled and shouted out, "Mami!" She turned in our direction, and we both waved to her. We embraced, and immediately, she said, "*I am so sorry I could not attend your wedding. It breaks my heart*—but it would have been impossible to attend both weddings, and this wedding had been planned for years ahead of time!"

"Mami, please, *we understand!*" Ricardo said. "And the only thing that is important is that *we are all together now!*"

His family was happy to meet me, and I felt welcomed immediately into their own. I loved his mami almost instantly, as she reminded me a great deal of Abuela. Ricardo's mami would be living with us in Pinar Del Río, and we would all be flying there tomorrow. Of course, I would miss my family very much, *having never been away from them,* along with the Isle of Pines, but we would visit often, *or so I hoped.* We still held out hope that perhaps Ricardo would be able to take a job at the university there; however, *he was doing so well in Pinar Del Río that it did not make sense for now to make any moves at all.*

The wedding was a grand occasion, and his cousin was beautiful, her new husband elegant, and both were quite honored that we had attended. Early the next morning, we left for the airport and the plane to Pinar Del Río. After a quick flight, a taxi took us to my new home. It was a fashionably styled, light-blue house with a front porch, two bedrooms, a modern kitchen, and two bathrooms, one with a tub. There was an expansive backyard with many jasmine trees which gave off the most wonderful aroma imaginable. *Another first for me was that we would be living in a neighborhood of the city of Pinar Del Río, and not on a farm!*

Chapter Six

I never knew that settling into a new home, and then keeping a home and household, would be so much work! *Of course, I did not mind a bit.* Right away, I realized that both Mami and Abuela had been great role models, and that most of the things I needed to do to run our new home had already been imprinted upon my mind. *I was happy*—Ricardo was working awfully hard, and yet he was such a loving and caring husband, and he frequently made time for just the two of us to go for dinner in town, walks about the neighborhood, or just spend lazy time together at the house. Pinar Del Río was a lovely city with its beautiful structures built in the Spanish colonial and mission tradition, tree-lined streets with benches and pots of flowers adorning most corners, and plentiful small shops owned by friendly families where one could find everything one needed. I enjoyed getting around by taking long walks downtown while learning where to get all the best bargains. Sometimes Ricardo's mami, whom we had decided I would refer to her as *Mami Natalia*, came along with me when she felt up for the walk. She was in very good shape at the age of sixty-five and had just begun the process of learning to slow down and find relaxing ways to spend her time, such as sitting on the lounge chair with a magazine or good book in our lovely backyard, or keeping busy in one of the seven small gardens we had around the yard.

I called home every week to let Papo and Mami know we were doing fine and to check up on my brothers and sisters. I missed them all greatly, and every week, we promised that we would soon make plans for visits there or here. Occasionally, Luis, Estrella, Fernando, or Lilliana would get on the phone to tell me what they had been doing and how much they missed me. I told them each they were always welcome to come out and stay with us anytime if they wanted to, at which point, I may have started the ball rolling with the youngest two, as Mami would then tell me they were forever hounding her about when they could come out for a visit. *Oh well, it would do me good to see them!*

Ricardo was still mentioning me almost every day on the radio until finally I told him he must stop; otherwise, I might become a local celebrity! *In fact,* the neighbor who lived in the house directly next to ours to the west on San Gabriel Street, *Enriqueta*, came over one morning saying she had just been listening to *Agriculture for All* on the radio, and that based upon the announcer's descriptions of his home, its location, and his lovely wife, she just had to check to see if the announcer was, in fact, Ricardo, *and I, his wife*. Reluctantly, I admitted that *yes, it was us.* She smiled and laughed and then I invited her in for coffee. Turns out, she grew up in Pinar Del Río and had been here all her life. Four years older than I was at twenty-seven, Enriqueta Delgado was just the same age as my brother Antonio, had been married for the past seven years to her husband Paco, who worked at the large cigar factory in town, and they had two boys—Sebastian, six, and Raul, five.

"The boys are at my mami's today visiting, *and so I have a rare morning off!*" Enriqueta said, laughing and then lifting her cup to take a sip of the fresh brewed coffee.

I learned right away that she smiled often and had an easy and contagious laugh which made me feel comfortable.

I told her all about my family and then Ricardo's doctoral program, along with his work at the bottling company and radio station.

"So, you are a seamstress. Good to know in case I need help mending some of the boys' or Paco's garments!" She laughed, but a bit more like a giggle this time around. "*In fact,* I believe I have seen some of your sister's work at the dress shop on Tenth Street. I recognized the name *Lilliana* immediately as you were telling me about your younger sister's work. Tell the truth—as soon as we can, I had been planning on buying one or two of her dresses anyway, *and now I have more reason to do so!*"

I smiled, and then found myself laughing a bit to accompany Enriqueta's. "Well, it seems we are both about the same size. If you ever need to borrow one of mine for the time being, *you are more than welcome to do so!*" With that, next thing I knew, I was showing her the dresses in my bedroom closet, and then listening to my new friend's wonderful ideas about decorating inside the house.

Over the next few months, I felt like I was fitting right in. Mami Natalia and I spent long hours in the kitchen cooking some of our favorite recipes to have for lunch and dinner. I packed Ricardo a lunch every morning, and he loved everything we made, *just like my brother Fernando would,* but especially my tortas, and so it was a pleasure cooking for him. Enriqueta and I began sharing various dishes when we made extra, and sometimes she would come by for a visit during the afternoon with her boys. They were both so adorable, playful, and fun-loving, and they reminded me very much of Luis when he was their age. We started having dinner over each other's houses every other week, and as I watched Ricardo interacting with the two boys, he was always so good with them. *I knew he was going to be a great father.*

Turned out, this was good for me to have discovered—*two months into marriage, I had a sign that something was unusual one morning upon awakening.* I was grateful for Mami Natalia for her care, knowledge, and wisdom, as well as for Enriqueta's. Ricardo and I had our first child on October tenth, and he wanted to name her after both his mami and me. *Angela Natalia* was so beautiful with a bright grin and loving hazel eyes. We began calling her by *Natalia* so as not to confuse with my own name. *Oh, I loved being a mom!* I had so much support at almost all times from Mami Natalia and Enriqueta, who both doted on her like she was their own. My baby Natalia was truly no fuss at all. Ricardo would come home after work, and the first thing he did each evening was check in on the baby. If she was awake, he would take her up in his arms and rock her for many playful minutes, interacting with her using happy expressions and a lighthearted voice. If she was sleeping, he would just stare at her with a peaceful smile on his face.

Soon after Natalia came into our lives, Ricardo had been offered, and accepted, a position at the soda company *Refresco* as floor manager, and his salary was increased by 7 percent. He had known the owner of the company, Edgar Narnia, from years before while they were both earning their bachelor's degrees, and Edgar gave Ricardo a position demanding a great deal of responsibility. He would be training and managing employees along with documenting their work conduct, as well as observing the efficiency of the production line, overseeing inventory and shipments, and ordering supplies.

We bought a used Singer sewing machine, which was in excellent condition, and in my spare time, I began sewing things for my and Ricardo's families and our neighbors. I had begun meeting more of Ricardo's family in time. His brothers Paquito and Leonardo, along with their wives and children, came for Sunday dinner about once a month and were quite fun-loving. His sister Margarita was quite handy in the kitchen and would always bake extra things to leave for us. Manuela, his youngest sister, worked at the general store I frequented, and she would always put aside items I needed and would tell me about the latest sales and fashion trends.

With events, occasions, and dinners sponsored by the radio station, the city, and the university, we were attending various outings frequently, and I enjoyed meeting and befriending Ricardo's colleagues and associates, along with their wives. Mami Natalia never minded watching the baby for us, and we felt secure knowing our little girl was in good hands. This changed a bit in that we did not go out as frequently, or attend as many events, after having our second daughter, Mary Antonieta, a year-and-a-half after Natalia. And then, even more so after our third child, Maritza, whom we called Marie, arrived late in the summer of 1956. Like Natalia, Mary and Marie were both such beautiful, happy, and healthy babies.

By this time, having earned his doctorate in education, and having made a name for himself with his broadcast, Ricardo had established himself among the elites and influencers of Pinar Del Río. He selected two of the most influential people in the city to be the godfathers to our two new girls—the mayor of Pinar Del Río, Juan Fernandez, and Congressman Sandalio Suarez. For Marie's baptism, we would be having quite a large gathering at our house after the service. *Almost my entire family would be coming out, along with much of Ricardo's.* I could not wait to see everyone as it had been a long time since we had been able to get together.

Although it would have been nice to have them stay at the house, it would have been much too crowded, and so my family would be staying at a hotel about ten minutes away. They were to arrive late Saturday and would go straight to the hotel, and so the first I would see them would be at the church for the baptismal service. A long caravan of autos and trucks would then drive us all back to our house. The morning finally arrived, and although it was to be a very hot and humid day, we had fans set up out in the backyard, and we had purchased a small kiddie pool for the young children. Otherwise, there would be plenty of cold beer and iced drinks available to fend off the intense heat.

It was difficult greeting everyone at the church as the mass demanded formality, but it was a truly inspiring service. *Finally,* outside the church right after, *I greeted my entire family, and it felt so wonderful seeing them all!* As I had instructed them beforehand, we would not have much time since we had to get back to the house and get ready for the large and celebratory dinner. No sooner had we said hello than we were back in our vehicles in the procession for home.

"How lovely everything is," Mami said. She looked beautiful, dressed in a new turquoise gown Lilliana had made for the occasion.

"Do you like the house?" I asked. We had just arrived home, and I was rushing to get changed and into the kitchen as Mami followed me. After putting on a light beige dress and my sturdy sandals, I quickly showed her the girls' bedroom and then the spare room we had converted into Mami Natalia's bedroom.

"I love what you did to everything," Mami said. "I can tell it all really has your special touch. Perhaps a bit crowded, but you've made it work. I'm proud of you, darling!"

It felt good to me knowing Mami thought so. We greeted everyone outside in the backyard, and I noticed that due to the heat, most people carried a damp cloth to wipe themselves down when necessary. Ricardo had hired a small, local band, and they were setting up with four musicians who would play guitar, trumpet, drums, and maracas. We finally got into the kitchen. My neighbors and Ricardo's family had prepared all the dishes ahead of time, and Mami and I began helping my neighbors prepare the platters. Introducing Mami to everyone—she was an immediate hit with my friends and fit right in. While getting everything ready, through the windows, I noticed the rest of my family out back mingling with Ricardo's relatives, and everyone seemed to be engaged and happy.

My girls were the center of attention for the first part of the day. Thankfully, Abuela and Mami Natalia had taken over child-watching duties. They seemed to be equally at ease with the two youngest girls, while my oldest Natalia was busy playing with Sebastian and Raul in the pool beneath Enriqueta's watchful eyes. I looked for Papo and saw that he was busy talking with Ricardo, Enriqueta's husband Paco, and with Ricardo's boss Edgar about something which required all of them to use dramatic hand gestures.

Papa Ramon strolled into the kitchen smoking a cigar and overseeing all of us ladies working diligently. "Some place, pumpkin!" He leaned over the counter to try a shrimp we had fried with coconut coating. "Umm—delicious! Your three girls are adorable." He came over to me, smiled, and pinched me on my cheek. "Happy to see that you've done quite well!"

I dropped what I was doing and gave him a huge hug. *"Papa Ramon, you were the inspiration behind all of my best successes!"*

He chuckled, and I looked back over to Mami and winked. As I finally began to unwind a bit now that, for the most part, everything was prepared and ready, I saw that my younger siblings had rounded up those their age and had started a game of soccer in a field behind our backyard. The afternoon progressed without a hitch and flew by. I decided I would get something for myself and then sat at the long table with Ricardo and my family with a plate full of food. Before eating anything, I took a moment to look around at both of our families, along with the friends and neighbors who had become so important to us over the years, and I relished the observation that everyone was happy, healthy, and enjoying our good food, drinks, and companionship.

Ricardo put his arm around me and gazed into my eyes. "You are amazing, my love!" He then smiled and leaned over to brush my hair from my eyes.

Not missing a beat, Fernando suddenly shouted, "Here's to Angela!" He raised his glass of rum and coconut milk high. *"The best mother, sister, and hostess Cuba has ever known!"*

Everyone at the table, and even most standing around or sitting at adjacent tables, raised their drinks and made comments supporting my brother's toast. Ricardo leaned in and gave me a gentle kiss. I blushed and glanced at Abuela for some reason, who was sitting in a lounge chair a few feet away, our middle child Mary sound asleep in her lap. She smiled and gave me a quick nod of support.

Poor baby Marie was exhausted. Mami had put her down moments earlier, and now she was sleeping comfortably in the crib beneath the tall, jasmine-covered cottonwood tree beside us, and could not know how many people had come out in celebration of her consecration to Jesus Christ.

As they had been most of the afternoon from my having casually observed their heated discussions and having overheard a few snippets of their arguments, Paco and Edgar were still debating politics as they sat drinking bottles of beer at the end of our table. I could tell it was a topic which had gained everybody's interests, and soon most of my and Ricardo's siblings, many of my neighbors, Papo, and even Ricardo himself had rejoined their conversation as they gathered together in a circular grouping.

"He's no good for us anymore," Paco said, looking intently into Edgar's eyes. "Ever since he had taken control back by military coup, and then even went so far as to cancel the 1952 elections, *Batista has gotten power hungry and no longer cares about his people."*

"I am not disagreeing with you," Edgar countered, tipping a bottle of cold beer back and draining half of it in one swig. "What you say is very true. Everyone knows he was a progressive during his first term, and then just when it looked like he would do our bidding, he has changed course and has proven himself far more to be a dictator than a president who is committed to his own people's needs."

I looked at Papo, who seemed to be waiting for the chance to say something. Instead, Ricardo's brother Leonardo, who was standing behind Edgar, intervened. "I don't know about much of all that, *but I do know* that our economy is suffering from such high unemployment, and that is not good for any of us."

Finally, Papo said, "I am concerned that Batista now has a blatant disregard for the things which would give us a better quality of life. Roads, clean water, farming subsidies…to me, he begrudges doing anything which might cost money, even if it would create a better life for most of us."

Sitting directly across from me, Papa Ramon added, "Seems he could care less about our farms and would let them go to waste in a heartbeat if it meant he could do some shady deal with the Americans in order to increase our imports of produce."

Edgar jumped back in. "As I was telling Paco just before, *American organized crime* made him rich and gave him too much, and now he cannot get out from beneath their grip. Their American companies completely dominate every aspect of our economy, and the politicians they hold within their grasp support Batista's dictatorship for all of these reasons."[2]

There was a silent pause which felt overwhelmingly heated, as if something unmentionable might just have been stoked. Everyone waited a moment in order to give it the chance it might need to create a smoky blaze which would embolden each of us.

It was my brother Antonio who sounded the first alarm. *"You are all missing the point, my friends.* What is truly going on beneath the surface of all that you speak, which is correct by the way, is that during his first term as president, Batista had not been supported by the Communist Party of Cuba. Since then, *he has become a devout anti-communist and that is why American interests support him.* Most of us would agree that this should be a good thing, all in all." Antonio looked across the table at Papa Ramon and then next to him at Papo, who were both fully engaged in hearing what he had to say. *"However, what Batista knows full well and many of us do not is that we have strong*

---

2 https://en.wikipedia.org/wiki/Cuban_Revolution

Communist persuasions in many levels of our society and government." He lifted his bottle of beer to his lips and now everybody waited on his next words.

Slapping the bottle down on to the wooden table, Antonio continued, "*They are giving him a hard time, and now he is growing very nervous.* In the months following Batista's 1952 coup, *this man by the name of Fidel Castro was only a young lawyer, but he was an activist who had petitioned the court system for the overthrow of Batista.* Only Castro believed early on that Batista's government was full of corruption and tyranny—most of the rest of us back then, and many of our supposed leaders, *turned a blind eye.* In his arguments against Batista, all of Castro's arguments were rejected by our courts, which of course, incidentally, *were overseen by Batista loyalists."*

It was Paco who seemed most inflamed by my brother's argument. He was next to command everybody's attention, and in a powerful voice full of excited condemnation, he shouted, *"Our courts sold us out, and now we have no recourse! After realizing that Batista's regime was not going to be replaced through legal means, remember what happened next?"* I saw that Paco's hands were shaking as he continued. "Castro basically informed the public that he was resolved to launch *an armed revolution.* They had tried once and failed, *but it is not over!* I know for a fact that he and his brother Raúl are coming back. They have stockpiled weapons and have been in the business of recruiting whoever they could find from the working classes. Face it, my friends—*war is coming one way or another, like it or not.*"

Edgar now nodded his agreement. "Yes, while we were all laboring our fingers to the bone, Batista was constantly pampering himself with exotic foods and elegant women. Something has to be done. This 26th of July Movement when he and his followers had begun their intention of overthrowing Batista, it has some grit to it. It had been on the twenty-sixth of July 1953, when they had first attacked the Moncada Barracks in Santiago and all of the barracks in Bayamo. *Castro will not give up so easily, and maybe that is a good thing for all of us!"*

I had known from neighbors and from the newspapers that many of the integral 26th of July Movement revolutionaries, including the Castro brothers, were captured in the mountains of the Oriente shortly after this initial assault in 1953. In the highly politicized trial which followed, Fidel Castro spoke for nearly four hours in his defense, ending with his now almost famous words, *"Condemn me, it does not matter. History will absolve me."* Castro used loyalty to a free Cuban spirit as his defense, and then had spoken about how the *non-elite classes* of Cubans needed better representation and government programs which would help to provide them with a secure future. It would not matter what he had said, since Batista controlled the judges. *Fidel was sentenced to fifteen years in the Presidio Modelo prison,* located on the Isle of Pines. His brother Raúl received a thirteen-year sentence.

Mostly due to Fidel's Jesuit childhood teachers persuading Batista to do so, in 1955, under broad political pressure, the Batista government had freed all political prisoners in Cuba, including the Castro brothers.[3]

Papa Ramon had been listening intently to the last part of the conversation. He grabbed his chin into his right hand and shook his head. "They, these Castro brothers, are now in Mexico with other rebels preparing for the overthrow of Batista, is that what you are suggesting, Paco?"

"Yes, they have hundreds of Cubans, along with several great commanders, many of them American, training them in all aspects of warfare. I know this is so because my brother is one of them."

Fernando had come back from the soccer game minutes before and had listened in to this last part. He said, "I have very recently read in an American magazine that last year, Fidel met with the *infamous Argentine revolutionary Ernesto "Che" Guevara,* and they have since banded together."

It bears mentioning here that Ricardo had one other brother whom I had never met, who himself had two sons and a daughter,

[3] https://en.wikipedia.org/wiki/Cuban_Revolution

and they all lived just on the outskirts of the western part of town. For reasons I was never made aware, Ricardo and this brother, whose name was Israel, never talked with one another, and we knew little about him over the years. However, one of Israel's sons, Ricardo's nephew René, had a reputation with his family of not easily being managed by his parents, and this had started early in his life.

Now almost an adult, Ricardo had run into him at the university on several occasions, and they had talked. Finally, one evening, Ricardo brought him home for dinner. He was a tall and lanky young man who seemed to me to be belligerent and angry at the world. Ricardo told me later that René had no permanent home and would stay here and there with various friends. We then discussed how we might help him, since it was apparent, he seemed to have no direction at all in life and he needed guidance.

Against my better judgment, we took him in right after he had gotten in trouble with the authorities for posting anti-Batista propaganda on electrical poles throughout downtown. Ricardo was determined to do the right thing and had always believed in going the extra mile to help others in need, and so we would try to help him in the best way we could. After the first few days at our home, I convinced myself that he just needed time to figure out what he would do with his life. René was helpful in a limited way around the house and with cleaning up after meals. I tried my best to see his good side, even though this was not easy at times, since he would take every offer of guidance as a test, *or worse, as an intrusion*. Many days during the week, even though he was not registered as a student, he would take the bus to the university, and several weeks after having come to live with us, he began taking entire day trips into Havana. Ricardo and I thought perhaps he was trying to decide if he wanted to continue with his studies.

One night after dinner, the girls had gone to bed early, and Mami Natalia, Ricardo, René, and I were back at the kitchen table after having watched the evening news. René began discussing Castro's 26th of July Movement because we all had heard the news broadcast about it on the television—*Castro and about eighty others, including his brother Raul and Che Guevara, had landed a yacht in*

Playa Las Coloradas. After a brief and failed skirmish with Batista's troops, the rebels had fled into and then scattered among the mountains of southeastern Cuba. Batista sent three of his best-trained and equipped regiments after them, and within hours, Cuba's Army had attacked and killed almost all the guerillas; although the TV reporter was not clear about how many, if any, had survived.

"I don't think Batista got all of them! From what I've been hearing from my friends at the university, who have a great bit of inside knowledge, at least four of the leaders escaped," René said. This was the first we had heard him discuss anything at all about what he might be doing all those hours spent at the university. Realizing he had now disclosed pertinent information about his own interests, he then continued. "I have been meeting with a group of students at the university who have ideas about how we can fix *all of the problems in our leadership.* They are a bright *and enthusiastic* sect of the university."

Ricardo sipped his mug of beer. He glanced at René with his ever-appealing, quizzical expression. "Well, it is good to know that you have some interests, René! Although, I don't know about this Castro, whom it would seem to me by noticing your excitement, that you have become quite a fan. Something tells me he is going to be trouble, *although I want to try to* believe he will be a good influence. His methods are unconventional, to say the least, and by doing the things he is doing, I just do not see how he will impose positive change."

René's tone turned adamant, and his speech became rapid. *"It's time we made some change or another!* Things cannot go on the way they've been going." He glanced at me briefly in order to see my expression, which I had tried hard to keep neutral, but was uncertain if I had succeeded. Looking back at Ricardo, he said, *"Don't you agree, uncle?"*

Ricardo was tired, and I knew at that moment that he just wanted to keep things relatively peaceful. *"Perhaps you are right.* I hope you are. Sometimes when I hear about the things Castro does in the name of Cuba, I just cannot see how we can assure he will impose the positive changes that he promises. Perhaps I feel the way

I do because the history of our nation supports the premise that we inherit one botched government after another, seemingly no matter what we as a culture, and as a people of goodwill, values, and principles, try to do…"

René smiled and shook his head thoughtfully. *"That is why the time has come for the people to take matters into their own hands."*

Mami Natalia finally spoke, and what she said had a great deal of wisdom to it, although it was quite depressing. "You men only want to take advantage of and then destroy things. There is no way we can have peace until a woman is in charge of everything!"

I had heard enough, as talk such as this only served to grate on my nerves. "In this part of the world, at this time, only men are given the opportunity to become our political leaders. But we shall see—*even men have to get things right once in a while!"* Everyone laughed except for René, who looked at me with a mixture of scorn and pity. Not allowing him to bring me down, I continued with my sentiments. "I believe we all need to stop letting ourselves become bothered by any of it! You both will see—we shall get it right once and for all. Our next leader will be the one who will stand up for democracy and for the people's rights, *and then we can have peace and harmony throughout our island."*

Mami Natalie and Ricardo both looked at me with a grin. René sort of glared at me as he lit his cigar.

After that night, I began paying very close attention to both René and to the news. It turned out he was right, and that the group of survivors in the mountains after Batista's troops had attacked the insurgents included Fidel and Raúl Castro, Che Guevara, and Camilo Cienfuegos. They had wandered through the mountains, looking for each other at first, until they had found the others and had regrouped. With the help of peasant sympathizers, it seems they were able to form a guerrilla army, and this had been their plan all along. On March 13, 1957, a separate group of revolutionaries—the anti-communist Student Revolutionary Directorate, or DRE, composed mostly of students from universities throughout the country—stormed the presidential palace in Havana, attempting to assassinate Batista and put an end to his government. I briefly worried if this had been the group which René had been aligning himself, but he would give nothing away. The attack had ended in utter failure with the leader of the DRE having died in a shootout with Batista's forces at the Havana radio station they had seized to spread the news of Batista's anticipated assassination.

While Batista continued battling various uprisings, a former American Army commander by the name of William Morgan began leading insurgents who called themselves the Second National Front, and it turned out, this group had close ties to the surviving members of the DRE. Morgan vigorously trained those under his command, utilizing the skills he had learned in the United States Army. It became apparent watching events unfold day by day, that Batista began to fear that his days were finally numbered. He began making drastic and unilateral decisions concerning Cuba's economy, by first nationalizing US oil refineries and then most other US businesses. He was now resorting to brutal and unethical methods in an attempt at keeping Cuba's cities under control. In the Sierra Maestra mountains, Castro and his army had begun staging frequent and successful attacks on small garrisons of Batista's troops.

I found myself buying and reading American magazines and tabloid publications. In one of them, it was reported that Castro had now been joined by a CIA-connected operative by the name of Frank Sturgis, who reportedly was assisting Castro and his colleagues in training the peasant troops in violent guerrilla warfare. Supposedly, Castro had accepted the offer of the CIA's help because he had an immediate need for guns and ammunition, and Sturgis had promised boatloads of weapons and ammunition from a CIA weapons depot in Florida. One newspaper went so far as to suggest that this Sturgis had even helped to open a vast and highly equipped training camp in the Sierra Maestra mountains, where he taught not only *the 26 of July Movement* rebel soldiers, but Che Guevara himself.[4]

Ricardo and I would discuss all these things, along with the politics behind them, on a regular basis. Not only us these days, but likewise, as did all of our family, neighbors, and the community at

[4] https://en.wikipedia.org/wiki/Cuban_Revolution

large. There was an uncertainty and even a looming fear over what was to come. We agreed that it seemed quite likely, no matter which way things turned out, that drastic change was upon each of us, along with our entire nation. Mami Natalia stayed on top of the news reports and our discussions at the beginning, but then, unfortunately, she had become tired as of late and would go to bed early. Then it happened one morning when she did not come for breakfast, that I had checked on her and found she had died during the night. She had passed peacefully in her sleep, and the doctors informed us that her heart had simply stopped beating. We had a full service for her at the church with Ricardo's family and our neighbors in attendance. This had occurred only a week before our fourth child, Olivia, came into the world. Also, I was glad when days later, René finally moved out and into an apartment near the university campus on the western part of Pinar Del Río.

Things occurred at a rapid pace thereafter. A pirate radio station called *Rebel Radio* was set up in February 1958, and it allowed Castro and his forces to broadcast their message of unity nationwide. On August 21, 1958, after defeating Batista's regiment sent in to destroy them, Castro's forces began their own offensive, and in the Oriente, they directed attacks on several different fronts. Descending from the mountains with newly acquired weapons, *Castro's forces won a series of victories and had begun to capture small cities and towns.* Meanwhile, several other rebel lines under the command of Che Guevara proceeded westward and confronted Batista's forces in that region. *Two of these battalions survived and were able to reach Cuba's central provinces, where they were joined by more rebel reinforcements.* However, here they also met anti-communist DRE forces, which had been fighting Batista's army for many months, and friction developed immediately between the two groups of rebels.

Castro's troops of guerillas finally ousted Batista on December 31, 1958, taking over the government buildings in Havana. News of this event caused Batista to panic, and he fled Cuba by air for the Dominican Republic early the next morning. Comandante William Morgan, the former American commander, continued leading the fight with the DRE rebel forces as Batista departed. Castro learned of

Batista's flight in the morning and immediately started negotiations to take over Santiago de Cuba. *On the second of January, the military commander in Santiago ordered his soldiers to stop fighting against Castro, and Castro's forces took over the city.* Castro himself arrived in Havana on January 8 after a long victory march, where he appointed his initial choice for president to be Manuel Urrutia Lleó, who took office on January 3.

Then horrors began. Almost immediately, hundreds of Batista-era agents, officials, soldiers, and policemen were put on public trial, accused of various crimes, including human rights abuses, murder, war crimes, and torture. *More than three hundred of those accused were convicted of political crimes by tribunals and then executed by firing squad,* while thousands more received life sentences of imprisonment with no chance for parole. After the capture of Santiago, Raúl Castro directed the execution of more than seventy Batista POWs without even as much as a hearing. Che Guevara was appointed supreme prosecutor in La Cabaña Fortress, the largest of all prisons in all of Cuba, and he routinely *gave life sentences and ordered the execution* of many other former Batista sympathizers, including civilians. Ricardo and I were astonished. *Fidel Castro obviously felt the need to prove a point while cleansing the entire government of Batista loyalists and potential opponents of his new government.*

In February 1959, the Ministry for the Recovery of Misappropriated Assets was created, *and Castro began expropriating land and private property.* He had a law enacted in order to validate this practice—*the Agrarian Reform Law of May 17, 1959.* Farms of any size could now be seized by the government, and many were, *while land, businesses, and companies owned by upper and middle-class Cubans were now being taken from them and labeled as nationalized property.* I worried sick for Papo's lumberyard and Papa Ramon's farm. For weeks I tried to call, but the phone lines were all down. On April 15, 1959, Castro began an eleven-day visit to the United States, at the invitation of the American Society of Newspaper Editors. Ricardo and I watched with disbelief as he said to the huge gathering of reporters, *"I know what the world thinks of us, that we are Communists, and of course I have said very clear that we are not Communists, very clear."* Castro said that he would replace Batista's government with a revolutionary socialist state. He proclaimed boldly, *"The equal right of all citizens to health, education, work, food, security, culture, science, and well-being—that is, the same rights we proclaimed when we began our struggle, in addition to those which emerge from our dreams of justice and equality for all inhabitants of our world—is what I wish for all."*[5]

When he returned to Cuba, Castro's government began a series of policies that had nothing to do *with what was in the best interests of his people.* In the name of nationalization and political consolidation, he soon transformed Cuba's entire economy. He created a revolutionary militia to expand his power base and then established the Committees for the Defense of the Revolution, *or CDRs.* Now, none of us were safe. At once, we all knew that CDRs were really another name for spies meant to monitor neighborhoods and inform of any counter or suspicious activities. Local CDRs were tasked with keeping a detailed record of each neighborhood's inhabitants, their livelihoods and spending habits, who their friends were, their level of contact with foreigners, work and education history, *and any and all suspicious behavior.* Persecuted groups were those who were very religious, educators, and homosexual men, and they were interrogated for no reason and often brought to jail with nothing more than having given a sour look to the wrong person.

For a while, we tried going on with our lives. Our fifth baby girl was born on May 15, 1960, and by all accounts, she was the prettiest and most congenial so far! We gave her the name Odalys, and now with five girls, we thought our family was finally complete. Finally, having gotten through to my family, they were all okay but had been given notice that their property was on the list for confiscation and had prepared themselves that this would happen sooner or later and were in the process of considering alternative housing. By the middle of 1960, Castro's new government had nationalized more than twenty billion dollars' worth of private property owned by Cubans. Not enough for his greedy little hands, *he then formally nationalized all foreign-owned property, particularly American holdings.* If anyone

[5] https://en.wikipedia.org/wiki/Cuban_Revolution

dissented, whether they be civilians or government officials, or complained when their property was being taken from them that they did not want to go and live in a tiny apartment, *they were immediately arrested, and many sent at once to the wall, where they would be assassinated by firing squad.*

"It's quite clear he is not a socialist *and that he is a blatant liar,"* Ricardo said as we ate dinner with our three oldest girls. The two youngest were sleeping together in their crib in the living room. "This is just what we had feared the most."

"Papo, why is he so mean?" Natalia, our oldest daughter and now nine years old, asked. Children could not be protected from news and discussions around the neighborhood regarding Castro's violence against his own people, and my oldest girls were constantly aware of occurrences and usually listened intently to our nightly conversations about government.

"Darling, I wish I could give you a justifiable answer to that," Ricardo responded.

Knowing my children were afraid of the leader of our country made me shiver with anger. *"We are headed for trouble, I fear,"* I said, wanting Ricardo to do something about it, but knowing there was nothing he could do.

Putting his fork down onto his plate, Ricardo said, "Cuba has come too far to end up with Communism."

Our second oldest, Mary, was still chewing her roasted chicken as she asked, "Why don't we move to that country Florida?" From years past, many of the friendliest visitors to our city came from Florida, and they were known, and greatly beloved, by the local children for being affable and having money to spend on things which they would sometimes give to the Cuban children.

"My pumpkin, Florida is just one state in the country of the United States, which has forty-nine more of them now since Hawaii and Alaska have just been added!"

Mary rolled her eyes. *"That's a big country!"*

"Papo and Mami, *maybe Mary's right,"* Natalia said. "If he is going to be in charge here, maybe we should go and live in the United States!"

I looked across the table at my husband, and I saw the pain in his eyes as he considered the wisdom of our daughter's words.

We had been lucky so far in that right after the triumph of the revolution, Ricardo had been sent to work at a new socialist company started by Fidel Castro named Viviendas Campesina, which literally meant *Peasant Housing*. He was in charge of sending out trucks with equipment, supplies, and guidance to help the farmers, mostly with irrigation needs, and had been recommended to the Castro regime for this role by university professors who had known of Ricardo's knowledge and experience in agriculture. With such duties as creating truck routes, overseeing truck maintenance and employee work schedules, procurement of equipment and supplies along the supply chain, and troubleshooting farmers' concerns as problems arose, *he always had his hands full.*

His direct boss was a gentleman by the name of Humberto Sorí Marín, and at first, my husband did all he could do to find out about Marín's past. Talking with his friends from the university and then the local officials we had come to know so well, who had only survived by pledging their loyalty to Castro, Ricardo was able to discover quite a bit about his boss, and he would relay the information to me in lengthy discussions over dinner those first few months on the job.

Dr. Humberto Sorí Marín was a Cuban revolutionary who had worked beside Fidel Castro during the revolution, and then after Castro took power in January 1959, he became the new Cuban Minister of Agriculture. In the early 1950s, Marín was a professional lawyer and a member of the Cuban political party Partido Auténtico, which had a very strong nationalistic ideology. *In 1957, he had joined the 26th of July Movement in the Sierra Maestra mountains, and he helped Fidel Castro to draft laws for Castro's burgeoning government regarding penalties for crimes, an official boycott of the impending presidential election on November 3, 1958, and agricultural reform, including some of the nationalization policies and procedures.* He had served in the rebel army, starting as a major, and then being promoted to comandante. He also carried the title of Judge Advocate General.[6]

[6] https://en.wikipedia.org/wiki/Humberto_Sor%C3%AD_Marin

Fearing he might be fired from his job, or much worse, if he let it slip out how much he hated Castro and his policies, *things became difficult for Ricardo on his new job.* He attempted to not speak about his opinions on Castro, or politics of any sort, to anybody from work. *Informants were everywhere, and you never knew who you could trust, and so the only option was silence.* Dissenters were being identified everywhere for very little cause, *and they were routinely found guilty of a made-up crime and then murdered at the wall.* Shouts of *Pa-re-dón* (*to the wall*) resounded throughout our country as Castro sympathizers, happy to be receiving free food and supplies, encouraged the ultimate price to be paid for former success of any kind.

I was at my wit's end. Fear and rage ran through me, and they were both combustible. When my tolerance limit could be stretched no further, one evening during dinner, Ricardo relayed to me an occurrence at work that day. His boss Marín had come into Ricardo's small office without asking, and then took the seat across from my husband's desk. Ricardo was very surprised, and at first thought he was in great danger, but before he could say a word, Dr. Marín said, *"I know your friend, the professor Dr. Lisbon from the university.* He speaks very well and thinks highly of you. I told him what a good worker you were, and then I wondered if you had patience for all of the warfare of the past several years. *He informed me that you were a very devout and loyal Cuban."* Ricardo nodded in silence as he tried to discern Marín's intentions.

Marín continued, "I, too, *am a fierce warrior* for a true Cuban democracy."

Ricardo stared deeply into Marín's eyes for a full measure. It certainly could have gone either way, but Ricardo reported to me that evening that it had been listening to my words to him nightly *about living under these horrible conditions imposed by Castro* which had helped him to make the choice right at that moment *that would forever change all of our lives.* Instead of backing away and remaining silent, Ricardo decided to trust Marín. He had seen him around other workers for months now and something in his gut informed my husband that he was a good man. So Ricardo said these words:

"This Castro had brought so much promise of finally providing us with a democracy, *but I fear it is not to be so."*

Thinking five soldiers were about to rush in on him, put him in handcuffs, and take him to the wall, Ricardo's heart was beating out of his chest as he waited for his boss's response.

Marín smiled suddenly, and then responded with, *"Yes—your words are true."* He waited a moment for Ricardo to register this offer of a bond of support, and the tension in the air quickly became a thick sizzle of energy. When he realized Ricardo could not wait to hear what was next, Marín continued. *"A company of good men for dinner, along with their wives beside them, would never arouse suspicion. Like-minded men have always come together when times required cause for deliberation. Perhaps we should plan a gathering presently to share some good food and viable discussion about the things which bother us most, in order that we might see if matters might be more justifiably served in other ways."*

Ricardo nodded. *And just like that…*

Our lives would never be the same!

Chapter Seven

The first of our dinners was a Saturday evening in September of 1960 at Dr. Humberto Sorí Marín's beautiful home in Western Pinar Del Río. His lovely wife, Antonia, was a gracious host and had prepared the most marvelous of feasts with the help of a few servants. Altogether, there were eight couples including Ricardo and me.

Two of the men worked directly with Ricardo at Viviendas Campesina, and they were involved with loading and driving trucks from the warehouse with supplies and machines for the farms. José Diaz and his wife, Bernita, seemed almost as equally uncertain as to the purpose of the dinner as I had felt as we gathered in the large parlor room adjacent to the dining room before the meal. The other warehouse worker was Jesús Corozo and his wife, Elena, who were jovial and had dressed very stylishly—he in a blue suit and her in an elegant peach gown. Two more of the men worked in a different section of the company and had not known Ricardo beforehand. They were mechanics who kept the trucks in good repair, and their names were Manuel Rodriguez along with his wife, Marisa, and Rafael and Isabel Domingo.

The other two men had known Dr. Marín from the Department of Agriculture and had been acquainted with Ricardo, as they each had roles at the university. Dr. Rogelio Perez was a sociology professor, whose wife was Beatriz, and they were both intellectually orientated. And finally, Professor Juan Cardona taught history and was accompanied by his wife, Yamilet. After cordial introductions in the parlor, we came into the dining room and sat at a very long table as the servants began to bring in serving trays and drinks. Throughout the meal, the conversation was lighthearted yet engaging. The men discussed American baseball, farming concerns with the impending harvest, and issues at the university, mostly regarding students' study habits and changes to the curriculum. The women contributed when we got the opportunity, mostly commenting on the beautiful home, how wonderful that we had all gotten together, and how delicious was the entire meal, but especially the ropa vieja. Still, I could not help the feeling that something more important was to come and, for now, was being avoided.

After dinner, Antonia brought the women out to the garden in the backyard, where we were served after-dinner drinks and given dessert of fresh fruit salad. It was a lovely evening, cool and breezy, and we sat comfortably on sturdy metal garden chairs with cushions. We finally had the chance to unwind from the tension, which I believe most of us felt regarding the uncertainty of the purpose for our gathering. However, it was difficult being blunt with each other at first, and so we engaged in conversations about our children, homes, and interests. As time wore on, it became increasingly obvious that each of us was dying to know what the men were trying to accomplish in the dining room, talking together so secretively. Finally, Professor Juan's wife, Yamilet, asked, "Does anyone know why our husbands seem bound and determined to keep us from the topic of their conversation?"

Nobody answered at first, until, looking to fill the void in conversation, Elena Corozo said in a demure manner, "Politics are so boring. Who wants to be bothered with such shenanigans? I leave all that to the men."

Bernita, the other warehouse worker's wife at the company, responded, "They are concerned with the direction our country is heading, Elena. Aren't you? I think it's quite important for all of us to keep up on current events."

Several of the other ladies agreed with Bernita's statement, while a few took Elena's side, thinking it best to stay out of their husband's affairs.

I listened and was not sure what to make of it all. Never having been one to avoid conflict, I waited for a pause and then interjected, "Antonia, do you get a feel from your husband just what they are discussing that seems to have such a sense of urgency?"

Sorí Marín's wife looked at me with a quiet confidence. She then briefly glanced down at her shoes for a moment before she answered. "Well...*my take is* this was just meant to be a pleasant dinner among some promising new friends." She glanced around at each of the ladies in turn. "I really don't know why some of you are thinking it is otherwise."

Yamilet seemed to take offense. "C'mon, Antonia! Although dinner is certainly a wonderful gesture, do you mean to tell me we have been sequestered out to the patio..." And then for reasons we were not immediately aware, she suddenly cut herself off from finishing her thought, and her eyes were glued to the window looking back into the house, which she then pointed at. "*And look*—now they have just closed the doors to the dining room." All the women turned at once to see that, in fact, the large wooden doors into the dining room had been shut. Yamilet then said with more conviction than before, "*Something is happening in that room,* that I can say with certainty. And I, for one, believe it is best if we women do not keep our heads in the sand *like a bunch of fearful ostriches.*"

We then looked at each other for answers. If anybody had any, they were giving nothing away, and so the conversation dwindled until we sat there silently, each of us worrying now what our husbands were so secretively planning amongst themselves. Shortly after this, the husbands broke out of their meeting, and we all realized how late it had gotten and began a pleasant round of goodbyes.

On the way home, Ricardo and I were silent at first. He then began asking if I had enjoyed gathering with the women and if I thought the house was as beautiful as he had believed it to be. I found myself remaining silent at first, and then finally, I said, "It was a nice evening. Yes, the house was gorgeous, and the food was great. I can't for the life of me figure out what you men were so busy discussing which required such privacy. *I am concerned, Ricardo.*"

"Just business matters, my love." When he realized by my expression that I would not take that alone for an answer, he added, "Mostly, we discussed if we could possibly do anything politically to ensure Castro does not go too far."

I was not sure if I believed him entirely. "Seems like any such discussion would be too little and too late, if you ask me."

He considered his next words carefully. "Sorí Marín has important and influential friends in America. He tried assuring us that if he were to gain enough support here, that he might be in a position wherein he would enlist their assistance somehow." He looked at me briefly and then turned his attention back to the road before us. "But only if things get much worse here. Anyway, the intention being finding some way to help our citizens if that were to be the case." I was not sure what to make of it, and before I could respond, he changed the subject entirely. "I still can't believe how glorious the house was. *Wouldn't it be wonderful having such lavish accommodations?"*

Two weeks later, we were at the house of Dr. Rogelio and Beatriz Perez for another dinner with the same group. This time, most of the women helped to serve the meal from the kitchen, and we all sat at two fold-out tables in the dining room. Once again, after dinner, the women departed for the living room, where we were entertained by Rogelio and Beatriz's son Aiden, aged nine, and daughter Elizabeth, aged eight, who showed us various drawings and science experiments. They were both very intelligent and confident children. After the children had finished, we watched the news on the TV while the men remained in the dining room discussing their agenda. An hour or so later, I was antsy and wanted to go home. Enriqueta had volunteered to watch our girls at home, and I did not want to leave her alone with my five children for so long. I silently got up from my chair and walked toward the dining room. As I got closer to the doorway, I heard one of the men saying, "...to make sure the timing of the truck's arrival coordinates with his breakfast," and realized it was spoken by Marín. Dr. Rogelio saw me approaching and he quieted the others. I looked at Ricardo and said, "My darling, we don't want to leave Enriqueta alone for so long. *We must soon be on our way!"*

I returned to the living room, and several of the women stared at me as I took my seat. I was grateful when, only ten minutes later, the men broke up and we said our goodbyes. Once again, on the way home, I tried to inquire about tonight's topic of discussion, but Ricardo did not want to discuss anything further about it. He seemed pensive and quite distant, and so I let it go. A few days after, he promised this would be the last of these dinners for now, but that we must plan on dinner for the group at our house in two weeks' time. Thankfully, Yamilet Cardona had volunteered to come out the afternoon before the dinner to help me get everything ready.

We had decided we would make sandwiches and have sides of fresh fruit, rice and beans, and salad. For the sandwiches, I had sautéed shredded pork tenderloin seasoned with paprika, garlic, black pepper, and light brown sugar. Yamilet and I then went into an assembly line of sorts as we layered each sandwich. For the bottom, we scooped out the pork, next added slices of cheese and smoked ham, and then a final cover of sliced pickles before adding the top. We then buttered the outside of both the top and bottom sides of the bread before frying them in a pan. Yamilet had heard how popular this sandwich had been for Cubans living in Florida, and it was her idea to try them tonight. We both kept a lighthearted and upbeat attitude as we worked and purposefully had discussed nothing about politics or the gentleman's cause. When Natalia and Mary returned from school, I had them do a taste test by giving them each half a sandwich. From the looks on the faces as they chewed, I knew the sandwiches would be a hit.

Finished with preparing the meal, and just before Ricardo was due to return from work, which would be only about half an hour from the time we expected our guests to arrive, Yamilet and I sat and had a cup of coffee. I could tell the time had come for her and I to have a real conversation about the thing which mattered to us most.

"These dinners seem to involve a high degree of tension," I said, sipping my coffee.

Yamilet smiled. "Yes. I know our husbands say that they don't want us to concern ourselves with their business, *but right now that is quite a difficult thing to do.*"

Nodding, I asked, "Do you have *any idea* what they are discussing or planning?"

She looked at me without answering for a moment. "Angela, let us right now make a promise to one another. *Let us agree to trust each other and to stay in touch no matter what.* Okay?"

Relieved to hear her suggest such a thing, I nodded vigorously. *"Of course.* That is a wonderful idea and a promise from me to you. *Whatever we share is to stay between just the two of us."*

"Agreed." She took a sip and watched out the window as Enriqueta was directing her boys Sebastian and Raul, now teenagers, as they washed their papo's bright green Chevy. Turning back to me, Yamilet said, "Don't get nervous or excited. *And don't tell a soul.* I overheard Juan speaking on the phone last week with Sorí Marín when he thought I had left to go shopping. Whatever is going on is being supported *by the American Central Intelligence Agency."*

December 18, 1960
Angela

Ricardo had left for work much earlier than usual. My oldest two had been up late playing, and since it was Christmas vacation and there was no school, I let them sleep late together with Marie and Olivia, who usually slept until about ten. I was just getting ready to make breakfast for all of us and feed my youngest, Odalys, who was sitting in her highchair, when I heard the front door opening. I picked Odalys up in my arms and ran from the kitchen to see who was coming into my house.

I was shocked to see it was Ricardo rushing into the house at this hour, since he never left work early. He seemed to be in a panic. I looked at him and said, "What happened? Why are you home so early?"

He stared at me for a moment, and I saw that sweat was beading across his forehead. I had never before seen the look I now saw on my husband's face, and immediately I felt ill. A mixture of dread, sorrow, and great loss all coalesced into a ghastly sight on one so fair. He came to me, touching Odalys gently on her tiny head as he said to me, *"I must leave."* At first, I did not know what he had meant, and I just stared at him. He reached and carefully took the baby from me, holding her tightly to himself. He then kissed Odalys very lovingly on her forehead. As I looked at him closely, trying to understand what was happening, my husband said once again, *"I need to go."*

I answered, still mystified with disbelief, *"What do you mean you have to go?"*

He said, "Angela, my darling, I have to leave and go hide for a while *and then try to leave the country!"* I could tell he wanted to explain more to me, and I stared at him, begging him to do so. He remained quiet, and I knew it was because he believed that *the less I knew, the better.*

I would have none of it. *"No!* You cannot leave me here with the girls all alone, *what am I to do?"* I took Odalys from him and held her in my arms.

He looked at me as if I had just handed him down the death sentence. "Okay, then I will stay, but if I do…" He lifted his right hand, extending his index finger and bringing it in a straight line across the base of his neck, as if he were to be beheaded somehow. I suddenly knew very well what he was indicating: "Pa-re-dón!" *The firing squad!*

"Oh, Ricardo, what have you done?"

He did not answer, and instead, he quickly dashed into our bedroom. I cried out, *"No!* Then, please, you must leave!" I began wailing horribly, and poor Odalys joined me. I wandered in circles around the living room and lost all sense of what I had been doing. The next thing I knew, Ricardo was coming in through the kitchen door, rushing into the house from the backyard.

He ran back to me and kissed Odalys once again on the forehead as I held her. He ran into the children's bedroom and then the spare room where Natalia and Mary now slept, kissing each of our four other daughters. I could hear them rousing as Ricardo ran back into the living room, and approaching me, he hugged and kissed me, then wiped away my tears. He looked at me with those familiar and piercing eyes, now full of determination, as he said, "*Be strong. I love you will all my heart.* If they come looking for me, tell them Odalys was feverish, and I had run to the neighboring city of Vinales to get a special medicine only available there." I could see the tears building in his eyes. "I will stay in touch, my love, and soon enough *you will know that we had tried for a free and democratic Cuba!"*

Through my flowing tears and cries of pain, I managed to say, "May God bless you and keep you safe. I hope one day we meet again, and if not, *your daughters and I will always love you and pray for your safety!!"*

December 18, 1960
Ricardo

There had been more than just a few men working at Viviendas Campesina who did not agree at all, or sympathize in the least, with Castro. Two of the men worked with me mapping out and ensuring the routes of the trucks which were loaded with farm equipment. The other two were mechanics, and of course, *the fifth man had been my boss.*

The mastermind of the plot was Dr. Humberto Sorí Marín, who it turned out, was in fact a CIA operative. He had enlisted the assistance of two tenured professors at the university since they had been instrumental to the cause through their academic influences along with the sheer power of their honor. Planning our dinners so that our meetings would not be obvious to the neighborhood snitches who worked for Castro, they always included spouses as to further the deception of innocent dinner parties. Ever since he had realized Castro was Communist, Sorí Marín had reestablished contact with the American Central Intelligence Agency. It had been his visit to the United States several years before wherein he had volunteered his assistance. It was the CIA who supported him in his mission and who had supplied the weapons we required.

During our first dinner, we declared that we would at first evaluate the severity of the threat which Castro had brought to our beloved Cuba before making any decisions about the course of action we would take. We openly had discussed Castro's legacy compared with what he had vowed. As each person contributed, it felt to me like we were holding court, *and that we were the jury and judges all at once.* The professors began by reviewing all his promises to the Cuban people.

In his 1953 "History Will Absolve Me" speech, Castro assured that if he came to power, the first thing he would do would be restoration of the 1940 constitution and a government of popular election. Castro's *manifesto* of July 1957 made another formal promise of general elections at the end of his first year in power, and he *absolutely guaranteed* freedom of information, press, and once again, all individual and political rights guaranteed by the 1940 constitution. His letter later that same year to the Cuban exiles upheld that the *prime duty* of the post-Batista provisional government was to hold general elections along with guaranteeing the rights of political parties during the provisional regime to organize campaigns. In an article in *Coronet* magazine of February 1958, Castro wrote of fighting for a truly honest general election within twelve months, and full freedoms of public information through a free press, and the reestablishment of all personal and political rights.[7] Professor Cardona concluded, "All his promises were like knives to the heart, proving just what he had done to make fools out of the Cuban people who had trusted him."

Dr. Sorí Marín then took over, explaining, quite angrily, that Castro had pledged the idea of grants of land to small farmers, along with the right of workers to share in profits. He said, "Castro's Land Reform Program had advocated large holdings for the agricultural enterprises while distributing unused land to farming families. When I had still been on Castro's team, he had defined his agrarian program as the distribution of barren lands and the conversion of squatters and sharecroppers *into proprietors of the lands they had worked on.*" He shook his head and sipped from a tumbler of rum. "The law I wrote and had signed, Law #3 of the Sierra Maestra on Agrarian Reform in October of 1958, was less than two months before Castro came to power and was based on the principle that those who cultivated the

---

[7] The Initial Aims of the 26th of July Movement. Approved For Release 2004/06/24: CIA-RDR79T00429A001400010010-0 From meeting of 13 November 1963

land should own it. *This law made no mention of cooperatives or state farms!* I, like so many other—*perhaps most*—of the original 26th of July members came to recognize too late that Castro had betrayed the revolution that brought him to power and had purposefully intended dictatorship all along."[8]

He had utterly failed in all fronts. We realized he had never intended even just one of these promises and had all along meant to establish Communism in our great country. He said what he had to say in order to gain the support of the lower and middle classes, *many whom he had allowed to give their very lives fighting for a cause that was always just a lie.* It had been during our second dinner that we listened to the final arguments. Between Dr. Marín's, Dr. Rogelio's, and Professor Cardona's testimonies, with near unanimity, they laid out how Castro's victory acceptance in January 1959 was not merely the result of his heroic struggle or his charismatic qualities; *it was because the ideas he had expressed and the promises he had made embodied the hopes and expectations of the great majority of the Cuban people and especially of the middle classes.* This was the result of the disappointments with the corrupt and aimless so-called *democratic* governments of 1944 to 1952 and the Batista despotism of 1952 to 1958. The Cuban middle class had been anticipating significant social and political reforms to make a return to the past ways impossible; Castro knew this, *and he capitalized on it by breaching their trust.*[9] The verdict and sentence were in!

It had been during the last dinner at my own house that we came up with the plan of how to impose justice, since there would be no taking him out of power without violence. Marín had already requested that the CIA provide us with guns and grenades, which they agreed to immediately, and they were smuggled in by a CIA operative from Nicaragua. The plot was to assassinate Fidel Castro at a restaurant he frequented for morning coffee and breakfast in Havana. Six of the men would be on the truck and would run in

[8] The Initial Aims of the 26th of July Movement. Approved For Release 2004/06/24: CIA-RDR79T00429A001400010010-0 From meeting of 13 November 1963

[9] Ibid

with rifles, guns, and explosives with the sole purpose of assassinating the Communist. Only Sorí Marín and I would remain behind the scenes. I would continue working at the factory as if nothing was any different that morning, and Sorí Marín would be in touch with updated information by radio communication to his contact from the CIA, letting them know how the operation was unfolding.

I had wanted to tell Angela everything, and I wanted her to be proud of what we were doing for Cuba. However, if we were successful, she would know soon enough, and if we were to fail, *then anything she knew could potentially kill her.* It was not worth the risk, no matter the price we both paid for my not sharing with her. It pained me greatly since I had never kept a single thing from my one and only love.

I had left for work very early. The plans were set in motion the night before with bringing the weapons in wooden crates into the warehouse and hiding them beneath one of the trucks. When I arrived at my post, all the men were already there. I saw to it that the truck they would be using was filled with the weapons, and I gave them all one final word of support. *"Know what you do today will be honored and celebrated by a free Cuba for centuries to come!"* They looked nervous but determined and nodded to me and then to one another. I patted the side of the truck and closed the back door. Walking around to the driver, Jesús, I gave him the thumbs up. He nodded and then put the truck into gear as he began down the boulevard.

Jesús had a handheld radio given to him by Sorí Marín from the CIA, which would permit him to contact Dr. Marín along the way. Not more than half an hour after they had departed, I had been waiting on pins and needles at my desk when Sorí Marín telephoned me. His voice was anxious and bereaved, and at once I knew something had gone horribly wrong. He said, "The truck was intercepted. It never got beyond the checkpoint on the border of Pinar Del Río. For reasons we never anticipated, the guards did not just wave it through as usual. They had sensed, or had been informed of a problem, and of course, right away they saw five men in back. The truck and all of the arms have been confiscated. *All six of our men have been taken into custody."* He paused, as if that were not bad enough. "Ricardo, they'll soon be coming for both of us. *They will know we were the only ones who could help organize, permit, and enforce this plot to kill Castro.* You must leave at once. *God be with you."*

I was in utter shock and felt a level of anxiety and devastation never before experienced. I was shaking, and my entire life flashed before my eyes. *It had all fallen apart because the extra men and the guns had been discovered in the back of the truck.* Immediately, I thought to go to my supervisor, who had been appointed to the position by Castro himself. I tried calming myself as much as I could and walked into his office and then told him that my baby Odalys had taken ill, *and I had to leave at once to rush and get a special medicine to bring home to my wife to administer to Odalys before her fever got worse.* He looked at me suspiciously, and for a moment I feared he had gotten word of the plot, but thankfully, the news did not reach him yet and he gave me permission to go.

I drove my auto as fast as I could, but without drawing undue attention, from the warehouse to home. Arriving back at my house under these circumstances was a terrible misery. *My last time coming home, and possibly the last time I would see my family.* Since it was still early morning, Angela was surprised to see me back home, at which point, she had asked, *"What happened? Why are you home so early?"* Once again, some part of me just wanted to come out and tell her everything. Then I would remember that by doing so, *I would be putting her life in jeopardy,* and so I remained quiet. Yet she had to know that I was leaving them *since it was a matter of my own life and death.* I told her if I did not leave right now, *that I would be going to the wall.*

I made sure to go into our bedroom to take out the metal box full of papers and money which I had put away months earlier by hiding them among my belongings in our closet. I quickly buried a meter into the ground beneath the flaming tree all the way at the end of our yard. I was hoping Angela had not watched me, since I did not want her to know yet where it was when Castro's goons came calling, which I knew they would. In several months, after the pressure had passed, I would inform Angela of its location, and she could then have money to use to buy things for herself and the children. The papers documented that Angela was officially my lawfully wedded wife, along with our children's birth records, and I hoped this would be enough for me to get them all out of Cuba and into America in the months ahead.

Holding my little girl and my darling angel one last time for now was all I could do, and it would have to be enough. I did not want to wake the other girls but had kissed them on their foreheads one last time while they still slept. *It killed me to leave, and I almost changed my mind, thinking I would confess and ask Castro for mercy. No! It would never do. The longer I stayed, the more I put all their lives in danger.* I ripped myself from Angela's arms, got back into my car, and headed to my destination—*the dry cleaners in downtown Pinar Del Río*.

I thought of death and dying the entire ride there. What good was it living in our beloved country as Communist slaves? *I had taken the noble route, and although it did not turn out as it should have, we had all done the right thing.* I did not want to die, although leaving my family behind felt like a kind of death. *The only solution was my own survival, so I could assure my family safe passage out of the hell Cuba had become.* Arriving at the dry cleaner's shop, I parked in the empty lot in the back of the building. As I got out and walked toward the front of the building, I was sure a blue Ford out on the boulevard had turned around once they had spotted me coming up the alley.

Mid-morning
Angela

I was completely beside myself. My daughters were wide awake now since Ricardo had intentionally slammed the front door on his final way out to ensure it was locked tightly. *I did not know what to tell them, and I wanted to call somebody—anybody—family, neighbors, friends, but what would I say?* I could not do so—*it would only implicate them through knowledge of subversive activity if they did not immediately report whatever I would tell them.*

Everything had so suddenly become such a mess and absolute disaster without any warning! I fell to my knees in prayer while still holding Odalys in my arms. Poor Olivia had just turned two and a half and was crying horrifically, sensing that something bad was happening. Both Mary and Marie had heard from Natalia that Papo had left for good, and they were walking around stunned and in a state of confusion. I finished my prayers quickly, asking God and the Blessed Mother for guidance, wisdom, strength, but most of all for Ricardo's and for all our safety and protection. As I was standing up from my knees, I went to comfort Olivia by taking her up in my right arm while still holding Odalys in my left. At the last second, as I was rising, she pulled away from me causing me to lose balance. Olivia went tumbling headfirst out of my arms, falling to the ground, and catching her left temple on the corner of the coffee table. Immediately, I saw a small open gash that began bleeding profusely.

I handed Odalys to Natalia and ran to the linen closet to get a fresh cloth, which I dampened with soap and water before applying to Olivia's wound. Just as I was getting everyone settled and was convincing myself that making breakfast for my children would be the best thing I could do at present, *there was a loud and commanding knock in the door.* My heart skipped a beat in my chest as I looked around the living room for any sign of Ricardo having just been home. A second later, the pounding on the door became continuous and threatening.

I smiled at my children and walked toward the front door. I tried to regain any composure left within me. Opening the door, to my utter consternation and dismay, Ricardo's nephew René was standing before me. He was dressed in the green Army fatigues of Castro's legions of assailants. *My first thought was the bastard had come to the house which had given him free shelter and nourishment not long ago with a full detachment of men.* Without asking, René came in, looking about the house, and he demanded to know if Ricardo was home and where was he. The armed *milicianos* goons in their green camouflage outfits, rifles slung across their backs and pistols in holsters around their waists, many of them smoking cigars, made their way through the house abruptly without asking permission. They ransacked the house. *I knew I had to put on the best performance of my life.* When René confronted me a second time, demanding to know where his uncle was, I put on as strong and domineering a voice as I could muster and shouted, *"I do not know!"* I looked deep within his eyes. "I have not seen him since he left for work."

He shouted so loudly the walls seemed to shake. *"Tell me at once!"*

All five of my girls were crying hysterically. The goons were in every room checking for Ricardo anywhere he might have hidden. Remembering what Ricardo had told me to say when they came looking for him, I said, "*Okay*—he is on his way to Vinales *because our baby Odalys is sick with fever and needs a special medicine.* We had checked in Pinar Del Río, but no pharmacies here carry it."

He sneered at me for a long and silent moment. I truly believe he would have slapped me if not for the presence of my children surrounding me on the floor already extremely agitated. *"And they only have it there?"*

"*Yes, René, it is true.*" And then I suddenly became inspired somehow to do something unexpected, which in retrospect, probably saved all our lives. *I went on the offensive.* "Do you honestly think he would be travelling all the way to Vinales for no other reason? Anyway, *why have you come for him?* Is he okay? *Has something happened to him?"*

He looked at me with silent disgust, and deep in the pit of my stomach, I knew I felt toward him every bit as much hatred as he had for me. I used the anger and rage I now felt, and it became easy for me to continue my charade. "*Please tell me!* Has he been in an accident, René? *Oh please, say it isn't so!"*

He gave me an unnerving stare, and I knew I had to go one step further to complete my affront. *"I had gotten word to him of the baby Odalys needing the medicine right away,* and he said he would rush to go get it and then come home! *Oh, don't tell me I have caused him to be in an accident with worry over the baby.* I would never forgive myself! I've been waiting for him, René, for over an hour—*and this just is not my morning.* Look—this one fell and hit her head, and now she's bleeding." I picked up Olivia and at once held her out to René, who backed up immediately.

Meantime, having exhausted all possible hiding spaces inside the house, René's men now went out into the backyard looking for Ricardo. Not knowing what else to do with me for now, René soon joined them, and I watched them talking among themselves for several moments. Two minutes later, they came back into the house, and René handed me a letter. He glared at me once again as he said, "Tell my Uncle Ricardo that he's done such a great job at Viviendas Campesina *that he is to be given a promotion.* They want to move him, and all of you, to Havana. *All expenses will be taken care of by Fidel Castro.* There are instructions in the letter."

I managed a smile and replied, "I will certainly tell him."

René then said, "Allow us take your daughter with the head injury to the clinic for you."

"No!" I replied, a bit too loudly, I feared. I calmed myself and went back into my role. "I know Ricardo will be getting home soon. We can just wait for him to drive us *but thank you!"*

Most of them left at that point, but I noticed several men waiting in the field in the back of the house, *and I knew they were there waiting to capture Ricardo.*

Mid-morning
Ricardo

I was glad that I had invented a plan B just in case it all went bad. For the past three weeks, I had gone over what I should do if anything went wrong, *which it had.* I had gone to the dry cleaner's to pick up a suit, a hat, and dress shirts, which I had left there last week for cleaning. As I waited for the proprietor to obtain my garments, I looked out the store's large glass windows and knew with certainty that someone in the blue Ford was watching me closely. *Or maybe I was imagining it?* They had parked across the street from the cleaner's and the windows were now up and had been tinted, so I could not see who was in the car.

I had planned coming to the cleaner's to not bring attention to leaving my house with any extra baggage. This would have aroused suspicion if the block snitches had observed me doing so. Going to the cleaner's was a normal and typical occurrence on my regular schedule. I changed my clothing behind the curtains in the dressing area at the front of the shop, telling the proprietor that I had a dinner event later and would not have time to go home beforehand. He told me to enjoy my dinner as I put on the fedora and pulled it down low on my forehead. Waiting for a family of two adults and three children who had just come in to get their clothing, I tagged along behind them as they left the shop, acting like I was one of them. *They did not even bother to notice me.* Not risking looking up, but keeping my head to the ground, I could not tell if the Ford was still there as I cut down the back alley.

When I got to my car, I locked my car doors, and then, leaving the car parked where it had been, I walked three blocks through narrow alleys to get to a bus stop out on the boulevard about a hundred kilometers south of the cleaner's location. Waiting nervously, I watched each car that passed by, expecting I would see someone who was staring at me, trying to identify me. I was grateful to God that so far, I did not see the blue Ford again. Finally, twenty minutes later, my bus arrived, and I took it into Havana. Nobody seemed to pay any attention to me on the bus, which was just fine. Once I got off, I walked ten blocks, trying not to look over my shoulder, but occasionally giving in to that temptation. Finally, I arrived at my last destination for now—*Angela's cousin Blanca's home.* We had met on several occasions over the years, and she was always very fond of me. She was very well off and had a beautiful house in Santo Suarez. Surprised to see me, she invited me in. Over coffee, and after catching her up on Angela and the kids, *I asked if she would take me in.*

She looked quite puzzled for just a moment or two. I was known and respected by most, and especially Angela's family, as always being helpful to others in whatever way necessary. I suppose one could say that I had acquired a reputation of doing right by others. I indicated to Blanca that it was in her own best interests not to ask me too many questions, that she could not let anybody know about me being here, and that I would be laying low and not heading out much. She was now single once again, her children were grown and out on their own, but especially because she had a hatred for Castro along with a flair for adventure, *she agreed immediately.*

Later that afternoon
Angela

I felt as if I had died. I desperately wanted to know what Ricardo and his friends from work had gotten themselves into, but especially, *what role Dr. Sorí Marín and possibly even the CIA had in the morning's events.* I wanted to call his wife Antonia but thought better of it, since I firmly believed *she would not tell me anything even if she did know.* I did watch the news, but since Castro's grip on our country took firm hold, our news was mostly fluff and not to be trusted, so there was nothing reported about any event in the morning as far as I could tell. When I remembered the promise Yamilet and I had made to each other, I ran to the phone and quickly dialed her number. *But there was no answer the three times I called.* I told myself I would try again later.

Hours passed. Thankfully, Natalia had taken over *mami duty* to all four of the other girls. She kept them entertained by playing inside and had even prepared lunch and then bathed them. Various noises throughout the day came to me from the men stationed in the field in the backyard. They would wander into the gardens directly behind our house. *I guessed they had decided not to bother hiding from me.* They took water from the spigot and some old fruit still hanging from the trees. I looked out the window occasionally to see them staring at me, and my nerves were completely on edge. *I stared at the phone, willing for it to ring, but it did not, and there was not a word from my husband or from any of the other wives.* As the sun was setting over our city, I saw four military jeeps drive up and park in front of our house. *My heart began beating so fast that I worried I would die of a heart attack right there.*

Yet my second thought *was relief.* For surely, by them coming back at this hour, it meant Ricardo was still a free man on the run, and this gave my heart rest. *They were here because they had not found him and wanted to harass me some more. I knew that I had to make an even better performance this go around!* René was leading the detachment of five others coming up the walk, and I decided there and then that I would hold strong and defiant in the face of *my nephew's interrogation.* I immediately marched to the front door, swung it open, and came out to the front stoop.

Putting my hands on my hips, I glared down at René. *"Do you have good news for me René, is Ricardo okay?"*

Ignoring me, he brushed by my side and entered the house. I turned and followed him in. Standing in the middle of the living room, he finally answered me by saying, *"Well, hasn't he been here?"*

I answered firmly, *"No,"* and then I really hammed it up. *"Has he been injured, and you don't want to tell me?"* I came right up to him face-to-face, fret and desperation covering my face. "Oh, René, please tell me and *don't leave me worrying so much!"*

The other scum went about the house searching. Natalia came into the living room carrying Odalys. She looked at René with disdain, and then she handed the baby to me before returning to the bedroom to be with her sisters. René peered deeply into my sad eyes and asked, "Did you get to give him the letter we had left earlier?"

"I told you he has not been here!" I ran to the window as if looking for Ricardo's car. "René, you must find him at once! *It has been hours and hours now!* I fear he has been in an accident and *maybe injured on the side of the road somewhere!* That can be the only explanation!" I began to cry hysterically while holding Odalys. *"Please find him and bring him home to me—you are his beloved nephew!"*

The soldier garbage returned to the living room shaking their heads at René, who then said to me, "If he shows up, *or if you hear from him at all,* you must tell us at once. Here is my number." He handed me a small slip of paper, which I took, intending to burn it later. *"We need to talk to him right away."*

Relieved when the other *milicianos* goons began departing out the front door, I stared at him with hopeful eyes and said, "I will, *of course,* let you know right away, René. You are his dear nephew, *and I would not want you to worry over your uncle's well-being."* I wondered if the ones out back would be leaving, as well, or if they were here to stay. "Keep me posted, my nephew, and don't forget to look in the hospitals, *or along the road to the pharmacy in Vinales just in case he had gotten into an accident."*

His hand had been on the pistol in his holster the entire time, and I breathed a long sigh of relief as he departed, got into the jeep, and accelerated down the road.

Chapter Eight

The next day
Ricardo

I woke up and thought I was living in a dream. Nothing seemed real and my environment was strange—the room, the sunlight, the feeling of separation from my family. I had to shake my head to clear the desperate feelings of doom and loss. Blanca had fixed a small breakfast of buttered toast and jam, and I was grateful for the strong cup of coffee. We did not discuss much, as she was weary of asking anything, and I of giving too much information away.

In my mind, I made a list of what I had to accomplish and gave each a number based upon priority. We had always figured phones were risky; however, Castro had not yet been able to infiltrate the entire phone system and so, though a chance, it was one I was still willing to take. I could not call home since that would be the first line likely to be tapped. And so, I called a brother-in-law.

Raul Fernando Concepcion was the husband of my middle sister Margarita. They lived with their two small children in Bejucal in the off-season and Havana during baseball season. Raul was a famous baseball player on the Cuban team the Santa Clara Leopards, and he was one of the best shortstops in the league. The Leopards were closing in on the championship this year, and so on the one hand, I felt like I should not bother him. Then, considering the desperation of my situation on the other hand, I knew I had no choice. I had known Raul even before he had married my sister, since he had grown up in Pinar Del Río and had spent his childhood working on a neighboring farm adjacent to the one we had worked long hours as a family. Due to his expertise on the playing field and his charitable lifestyle,

Raul had garnered many important contacts who had aligned themselves with him over the years. Since he had always looked to go to America to play, he had made connections from both the United States and Uruguay, which more than most other Latino nations, had spotty influence with the Cuban government over the decades. It was well-known that the Uruguayan government would occasionally assist Cubans through diplomatic means to come to South America or the United States.

Boy, did I need him now, along with his potential contacts!

Rumor had it, direct from Sorí Marín, that the CIA would often recruit some of our best ball players, eager to develop rapport with American interests, in order to help with their intelligence and their agenda. If anyone would have taken the bait, it would have been Raul, since he hated the dictatorship of Batista, and now even more so, *that of Castro*. I had memorized Raul and my sister's phone numbers both in Havana and in Pinar Del Río as soon as our plot was finalized during that third dinner. Blanca showed me the phone and then excused herself to go outside and do some gardening.

My sister answered on the fourth ring and recognized my voice immediately. *"Hey, brother! Such a funny thing—I was just thinking about calling you and Angela to see about getting together once the season is over."*

"Hi, Marge!" I had prepared for this eventuality. I did not want to raise any questions or give her cause to worry, and yet, I needed to get right to the point with her husband. "Yes, that will be just great! I will tell Angela to give you a call next week. How is everyone?"

We made small talk and finally, I said, "I need to speak to your husband regarding a baseball matter. Trying to get some seats to one of the playoff games. *Is he home?"*

"Yes, you just caught him. He'll be heading out to the stadium soon. Hold on."

A moment later, Raul came on. *"How is my favorite brother-in-law?"* His voice was warm and confident, and hearing it immediately brought me relief.

"Raul, I have an urgent matter. *Don't let Marge know a thing.* I need to meet you at the stadium, today, before your warm-up."

I was met with silence. Then, finally, Raul's voice came back. *"Okay. Come to the players clubhouse at two pm and tell the doorman Juan to get me."*

"Thanks, Raul. I'll need twenty minutes of your time."

"Sounds important. You got it."

The next listed item on my agenda was thoroughly changing my appearance. Blanca cut my hair out on the back patio quite short, and then we dyed what was left using one of her brown hair dyes. She then trimmed my moustache, and using the growth already flourishing around my lips and cheeks, we began to fashion a goatee, which we then, of course, dyed using the same coloring we had for my hair. Altogether, I now had a decidedly mahogany look. I took some of her son's casual clothes left in the dresser of the spare bedroom which I now occupied, for his use when he would come to visit. Some of the things, like the T-shirt and baseball cap, were distinctly American, and overall, when I looked in the long mirror behind the door, I thought I could easily pass for a tourist from the United States.

Blanca approved my look and gave me the keys to her car, which I drove to the stadium. I felt funny due to my new looks, and yet extremely worried at the same time—*quite a combination.* I had one eye in the rear-view mirror the entire drive, but thankfully, I did not spot any suspicious or trailing vehicle. I made it to the stadium, and it was hours to go before the game, so there was a parking spot close to the players clubhouse. The doorman Juan was dressed in black pants and an official blue Santa Clara Leopards' button-down shirt. He seemed to be expecting me and nodded a greeting. "Wait here."

I tried acting casual as several other players, along with stadium staff members, passed by. Two minutes later, Raul came out the door to the clubhouse, tall and muscular and wearing the Leopards' warm-up sweat outfit. *He gave me a doubletake before realizing that it was, indeed, me.* "I would have thought you were a cheesy American tourist waiting to get autographs!" I smiled faintly, and seeing my expression, he said, "I am assuming we will be needing the assurance of privacy." I nodded. "Come this way." We went down a cement walkway toward the bathrooms and concession area. We then cut outside and came around the back of the stands until we stopped somewhere between home and third base. "Trust me when I say that, *from experience*, I know this is a safe spot. Nobody can overhear us."

Nonetheless, I looked in every direction around us and seeing nobody close by, I laid it all out for him—*from day one with Sorí Marín in my office at the warehouse, to saying goodbye to my family, and all the way to arriving at Blanca's doorstep yesterday.*

His next words would shock the hell out of me. *"They are all dead, Ricardo."*

I stared at him, uncertain at first. Then I realized he had meant all six other men who had committed to the plot and had been captured in the truck at the checkpoint. My heart sank to my feet.

"Four murdered at the wall yesterday evening, and the other two at sunrise this morning. It is not general news yet, but my contacts are to be trusted. *I had no idea you had been involved.* We knew it was someone else from Viviendas Campesina, *and I should have guessed it was you and called Angela to find out if she and the children were okay."* He shook his head and smiled at me with a mischievous grin. "That lucky son of a bitch! You could have had him, and it would have changed the course of our country! *Why couldn't it have been?"* Now, his face was filled with concern. "Marín is alive, thank God, and I believe he will try to get to the United States with help from his friends there."

I could wait no longer. I needed assurance he was going to be of assistance to us. *"I need a favor*—go to Angela as soon as you can. Let her know I am okay and see if she and the children are all right and if they need anything."

I was so happy when he did not hesitate in the least. *"Of course.* With Christmas next week, we have a break after tonight's game. I can go first thing in the morning."

I nodded. "Probably best if we don't worry Marge about any of this."

"No, of course. Do you know what you are going to do?"

"I was hoping Sorí Marín would get the CIA to help me and my family out of Cuba until Castro can be disposed."

He shook his head. "After this incident, *Castro will cut whatever is left of American relations to the bone.* He will know the weapons were channeled to you through the CIA. I have a better idea." We discussed an alternative solution that seemed like it might work. *After all, what did I have to lose?*

I changed the subject momentarily to baseball. *I do not know why I did this, but I did*—it just seemed a fitting way for Raul and I to bond as two regular men once again. "You play *Cienfuegos* tonight. You will probably have to face off with them in the series."

"Yes…they are good. *Luis Tiant, Junior, is unhittable.* His fastball is respected across the league. Really, it's stunning to see."

"He pitches tonight?"

"No—Ramos." I thought he would act relieved, but instead, once again, he shook his head, but this time in a forlorn manner.

"What's the matter now?" I asked.

"This is it. You will soon hear it—word has come down that after this season, *Castro is shutting down all professional baseball."* I was shocked and did not imagine even that Castro would go so far. "Many players are planning to get on whatever floats in order to get to the USA. Some are heading to South America. *I don't know what to do with Marge and the kids, Ricardo.* Very tough choice."

"I can't believe that bastard is ending baseball."

"He may have an all-amateur league, but that is little consolation when you've spent your entire life training, doing nothing else, just to earn enough money to support your family." I nodded. "Listen, my compañero, you sit tight *and don't go out!* Don't worry about Angela and the girls, *I've got them covered!* I will call as soon as I get home tomorrow night, and don't call Angela no matter how much you may be tempted. *Much too risky for all of you.* I will tell her your sentiments. Also, I will begin making the plans we discussed for your survival. You'll be okay."

I thanked him profusely, and before departing, I said, "When you call me at Blanca's, refer to me as *Lolo*, as in short for Rolando."

He tipped his cap to me, turned, and though I did not know it at the time, that meeting would be the start to securing whatever future was left for me and my family.

The month following
Angela

I was barely surviving at first. The uncertainties of what had happened to Ricardo, along with what would happen to my family, were like knives to my heart, stabbing and killing me each and every moment of the day. *My daughters missed their father and that is just something a mother cannot fix.* I felt like an alien being having landed on earth all by myself, since I could not tell a soul the truth about what had happened and what I knew. Because Castro's goons had made such a show of their presence in my home, Enriqueta and her family were now afraid of associating with me. I had hoped that Yamilet, and all of the other wives, had somehow survived this crisis, and yet I instinctively knew that, like me, she and the others would be too afraid of further implicating themselves should they make contact with any of the rest of us.

It was hell on earth, plain and simple.

I began to consider the strong possibility of informing Ricardo's youngest sister, Manuela, along with her husband Alberto Rodriguez, about the truth of what had transpired. They were my best hope for telling anybody the truth if I were to enlist anybody's help and support. I felt *almost entirely* confident that I could trust them, since Alberto and Manuela had always been so outspoken about hating dictatorship for Cuba and wanting democracy. *This is the same Alberto Rodriguez who had owned the hardware store in Pinar Del Rio.* Manuela's love for him proved too strong, and they had found a way to conquer the distance between them, falling in love and marrying years ago. She had convinced him that he would do better business in Pinar Del Río, and so they set up a home here, and the two of them started a new hardware store downtown just last year. *I will call them on Wednesday if I have not heard from anybody by then.*

On Tuesday morning, getting the children ready for the holidays and having absolutely no idea about what I was going to do for Christmas all by ourselves, I heard a knock on the door. I realized at once that it seemed like a friendly knock and not the threatening ones of René. *I peered out the window and could not believe it!* Opening the front door, I was happy to see Ricardo's middle sister's husband, Raul, suddenly standing outside on the front patio. A famous baseball player, I was shocked to see him at my door so unexpectedly. He tipped his cap to me, "Hi, Angela."

"Raul, what a pleasant surprise!" I peered at him a moment longer than I should have, trying to discern his intentions.

Still smiling at me, he asked, "Can I come in—*we have to talk.*"

"Of course!" I welcomed him into our home, and the first thing he did was to pick up each of the girls, who had come to greet him with a hug. They were so happy to see him, but before they could talk to him about their dad, I had Natalia whisk the other girls into the bedroom to play with their dolls. Raul and I sat down at the kitchen table, and I brought over two cups of hot coffee. I was quite curious and also nervous as I considered the possibilities of what he had come to discuss.

As soon as I sat beside him, he immediately leaned close to my ear, and in a hushed whisper, the first thing he said was, *"Are there any of Castro's soldiers about?"*

I peered deeply into his eyes and all at once, I knew that he knew. I glanced out the back window, and he followed my gaze and then immediately stood. In his normal voice, while walking over to the windows and gazing out back, he asked, "How have the girls been, Angela? It's been so long since I've seen them, and they've grown so much."

As I responded to him, he opened the back door and began walking outside. "Ah, yes, I love your backyard so much. *The flowers and trees are magnificent!* While you finish cooking whatever it is you have boiling there on the stove, let me take a look at *what you've done back here.* I will be right back!"

There was nothing cooking, but I went along with it and went to the stove and made believe I was stirring an empty pot. When he returned about five minutes later, he said, "Let's talk low. It looks like you are all clear here, *but we can never be sure.*" I pulled my chair close to him and immediately felt my stomach tumbling as I considered what Raul might be telling me. He saw the look of dread on my face and said, "I know about Ricardo and the entire plot." I knew right away that this would be too much for me. *I could listen to no more!* I was still furious at Sorí Marín *and what he had done to get my Ricardo involved.* I stood up and put my hands to my stomach. Seeing my reaction, Raul stood. He pulled me close to him, and with his arms around my back, he patted me on the shoulders. "I saw him yesterday, *Angela—he is fine!"*

I screamed out with joy, and then broke down and began crying uncontrollably.

The girls came running out, and I held each of them to me in turn, telling them that their papo was okay. Dismissing them then back to their room, I told Raul that *I could listen to no more on my own.* I told him my idea about informing Manuela and Alberto about everything, and of course, Raul had known them both very well. He agreed with me that it would be safe to have them involved, and so I called them at the hardware store. *Upon hearing the desperation in my voice, they drove over to the house immediately.* We all shared everything together, and as we had hoped, they took it all very well.

The rest of the week passed a bit more easily. I kept a watchful eye for either René or any of the milicianos, but other than an Army jeep parked on the street a block away from the house every day for several hours, nobody else came to the house. I took a bit of comfort knowing I now had Raul, Manuela, and Alberto on my side. During the thorough discussion that morning, I discovered Ricardo was staying with my cousin Blanca in Havana, and that Raul was going to try using his contacts to get Ricardo into the Uruguayan embassy, where presumably, he would be safe. Together, the three of them insisted that they would raise money to help support me and the girls for now, *and start putting some away as they tried to find a way of getting Ricardo out of Cuba for good.* Unfortunately, I had also heard from Raul the fate of the other six men. He believed so far that all of the wives were okay and had just discovered that morning that Sorí Marín had been able to escape to the US through his connections with the CIA.

Sure, he got my husband and the other men involved knowing he would have safe passage out of Cuba ahead of time if things went bad—

all the while knowing he would be sacrificing the other men, including Ricardo, by not bothering to ensure their escape route!

Before they had departed at lunchtime, Raul strongly advised me to not get in touch with any of the other wives, and Manuela and Alberto promised to come over Christmas Day to give the girls some gifts and to spend a few hours visiting with us. Finally, Raul had said that once Ricardo was safely in the embassy, that we could perhaps find a way of seeing him from the road, but that he would have to think about it some more.

By the second week after the failed assassination attempt, I was slowly beginning to recover. Having affirmed within myself to stop my self-pity and *to pull myself up from my bootstraps, as they say,* I became determined to make the best of things until we could find a way to be reunited in time. I was now always exceedingly cautious with everything I or the girls did. I figured Castro's men had concluded that I had not known about, *or had any part in the plot,* and that was what had saved me so far. Hopefully, the other wives had fared as well. I did not contact my family for now. *When the time came, I would simply tell them Ricardo had been assigned work by Castro's government on the other side of the island.*

My first order of business was learning to drive, getting a car if I could, and then finding a way to make some money. *Abuela's secret recipe for guava marmalade had always been a back-up plan for me as far as a business of my own.* She would make it every year at harvest, and it was always a hit with family and friends! Then, during the middle of the third week on our own, I received a strange box at my doorstep that had been delivered by a private courier early in the morning. It had the baseball team, the Santa Clara Leopards, as its return address, and the box itself had the emblem of a gift shop in Havana. I opened it immediately and found it was a box of those gummy cherry candies I had loved so much from childhood. *Only Ricardo had known about those!* I took the clear plastic package of candies from the box and beneath it, at the bottom of the box, was a letter. Unfolding it, I saw at once that it was a note written in pencil and in Ricardo's handwriting:

> We must be diligent and prepare ourselves for leaving soon. Much better times to come. I will always love you and the girls and can't wait to see you soon!
>
> Yours—Lolo!

Next several months
Ricardo

I stayed at the safe house for a month with my new makeover and under the name of Lolo. I barely went out of the house and had noticed that during the past two weeks, there was an Army jeep which drove around frequently throughout the neighborhood. I watched closely every time I could, praying they did not stop at Blanca's house. Raul came to visit on two occasions altogether late in the evening. He had assured me Angela and the girls were safe *and that my sister Manuela and her husband Alberto were watching over them closely*. During the second visit, I gave him a note for Angela that he assured he could have delivered to her safely. He gave me a date and the instructions about what I should expect.

At six o'clock, on the evening of January 21, 1962, I told Blanca how much I had appreciated her hospitality, along with her loyalty, and thanked her for having given me shelter for the past month or so. She smiled, gave me a hug, and then told me to take care of *myself, Angela, and the girls.* I nodded and then waited by the front door with nothing on me but the clothes on my back and a few items in a small pouch which I had attached to my belt.

At precisely six fifteen, I watched as a long black sedan pulled up in front of Blanca's house. Its windows were tinted, and otherwise, in the dark of the night, I could see nothing more until the passenger door clicked open. I immediately opened the front door of the house and ran into the sedan, firmly slamming the door shut behind me. Before I could say a word, the car began moving forward and down the street.

"Welcome to Uruguay," I heard a voice coming from the back seat. I turned to see an older man dressed in a tuxedo, along with a beautiful woman in a red evening gown. "I am Ambassador Bruno Rodrigo—*Uruguayan Emissary to Cuba*. This is my girlfriend Cynthia. Allow us to escort you to our embassy and keep you safely until such a time we can make proper arrangements for you!"

I nodded, and then for the first time in over a month, I smiled.

Angela

Now that he was at the embassy and no further interrogation had come from any milicianos, I was able to breathe a bit easier and concentrate on caring for the girls and earning money. On a Tuesday in early February, along with Ricardo's youngest sister and with my oldest and youngest daughters, I got into the back seat of Alberto's Ford Tudor, and we made the two-hour trip from Pinar Del Río to Havana. I was so excited and more than just a little nervous. Our cover for the trip would be that we were going to purchase extra learning materials for Marie at a specialty store in Havana. *In reality, we were going to see Ricardo at the embassy!*

Not that we would actually visit with him. *Much too dangerous.* Instead, as we got a taxi who circled around the embassy, we would catch Ricardo, or should I say *Lolo*, standing on the porch of the embassy from the third floor of the building, looking down at us. After a long, two-hour ride, we finally reached the embassy. I rolled down the window and held our baby Odalys up to it for him to see her. The driver became quite nervous when I did this. He said, *"Be careful not to draw attention to ourselves! There are eyes all around us!"* As we approached the very front of the building, *I saw him at the porch ledge*. I could not believe how Ricardo looked—his appearance was completely different, *and I kind of liked it!* "Odalys, there's Papo," I said. Then, my oldest daughter climbed on to my lap to get a view.

He waved the white handkerchief held in his hand, smiling, and I could see the look on his face. *I knew my husband was so happy to see some of his family*, even if only a drive-by. We had agreed beforehand through communication with Raul that we would only come around for four passes altogether, as any more than that would certainly increase exposure to all of us with the milicianos.

Ricardo

Seeing Angela and my girls down on the street lifted my spirits immensely. I could not wait to get them back with me, and *I would work with all effort, tirelessly, and doing whatever it would take to be reunited with my family.* Tears came as I considered the beautiful face of my baby daughter Odalys, and I could not stand the thought of even another day separated from any of my children. From what I could tell, Angela looked good—*strong and determined.* I used the handkerchief in my hand to dry my tears, and when they took the final lap around the block and drove by for the last time, I would have done anything to convince the embassy to take them all in right at this very moment.

However, there was only so much influence Bruno Rodrigo and the Uruguayan government could exert over Castro's government. If they tried to ask for too much, it would come back on them in various and sordid ways which were often very costly. *I prayed and tried to remain patient.* I knew that the US government was extremely interested in me, and that they were trying to have a hand working with Uruguay in the plans for my future, although the details were not being made known to me. Over the past couple of years, I had developed diabetes, and medical care at the embassy, although sufficient, was not meant for daily monitoring of blood glucose levels or the ongoing treatment with insulin. *Due to this and other things, there was now a sense of urgency to get me out of Cuba.*

I got occasional reports from Raul regarding other plans on ridding Cuba of the terminal disease which Castro's infection had caused for our country. He could not give me specifics but made mention of Sorí Marín having been involved once again. *I was ever so troubled upon discovering that none of the plots had thus far been successful.* I continued writing Angela once per week and would have increased my frequency but did not want to put her and the girls at undue risk. Anything which became too obvious became suspect, and interrogation or worse would soon follow. And then without warning, one morning in the middle of May, I was informed that within a matter of twenty minutes, and with the assistance of the CIA, I would be leaving Cuba and flying to Merida, Mexico. I was handed documents and given a wig of black hair along with a hat, leather boots, and overlarge sunglasses. Putting all of these things on, I felt absolutely ridiculous.

The last thing Bruno Rodrigo said to me as I was escorted through the back door and into an old four-door Chevy Deluxe was, "*Under penalty of immediate arrest and a sentence of life in prison, you are to disavow all knowledge of any American assistance, especially their CIA, for the remainder of your days.* Have a safe trip, and it's been a pleasure!"

May 1961–December 1966
Ricardo

I was taken to the Jose Marti International Airport with a fake Uruguay passport, stating I was Sebastian Rodrigo, presumably a relative of the ambassador. Out in the open once again for the first time in nearly five months, I was a bit paranoid and figured a battalion of soldiers in those ugly green army fatigues, with machine guns wrapped around their backs and long cigars dangling out of their mouths, would descend upon me at any given moment and *I was going to be arrested and sent to the wall.* During the drive to the airport, the driver did not say a word to me. I kept looking behind to see if any cars were following us, and I tried to discern from where an ambush of milicianos jeeps and soldiers might be coming to descend upon us. I checked my look in the rear-view mirror and did not recognize myself. I looked like a real American from the plains of

Mid-America. The driver had noticed my anxiety and just looked at me through the same mirror and calmly shook his head. *All the while, I did not believe I was free of Castro's murderous grip.* Even after we parked, my legs begrudged lifting my body from the relative safety of the vehicle and then moving it across the asphalt to the terminal. Yet, even so, somehow the driver was able to escort me into the terminal and to the correct gate, *my hands trembling and with a racing heart.*

I boarded a commercial flight to Merida, Yucatan, Mexico. Up until the moment the plane took off, I worried. Even when in the air, I was afraid that the plane would be hijacked back to Cuba where I would surely face *paredon.* I suppose somewhere, once we had crossed the sea and were over land again, I had finally come to believe that perhaps all of the efforts of the US and Uruguayan governments, Raul, and Ambassador Rodrigo *would be successful.* I began dreaming of Angela and the girls being rescued safely and returned to me. Though nobody had confirmed it, I figured we would wind up in the United States. This idea was supported once we had landed in Merida.

As soon as I came down the staircase from the plane and on to the tarmac, I saw two Anglo men in business suits standing side-by-side, and they seemed to recognize me. As they approached me, my first instinct was to run, but then right away I could think of no possible way Castro would have such white-skinned friends. They introduced themselves and showed me badges identifying themselves as US consular officials. They escorted me to a private room within the airport, where they asked me all sorts of questions about Dr. Humberto Sorí Marín and our failed plot. At first, I was hesitant to answer, and then I remembered Angela and the girls and soon became motivated to give them *any and everything they needed.* Two hours later, we had finished, but then I was interviewed by three agents of the Federal Bureau of Investigation, the famous FBI, *where I repeated for the second and then third time all the same information.* The agents had been nice enough and extremely thorough about every little detail. Eventually, they signed and stamped endless piles of paper and told me I would be processed and approved for forward travel to the United States.

On several occasions, I had asked both sets of officials if they could please help get my wife and five little girls out—that they might be in danger and in any event, they needed their father to care for them. They placated me by suggesting it was in the works; *however, I never got a definite answer.* It was frustrating for certain, but there was nothing I could do. If I caused too much trouble, I was sure they would wash their hands of me, *and then what good would I be to anybody?* I remained in Mexico for three days at a safe house run by the American consulate. It was guarded by soldiers, and I got my first taste of American food and American culture. I had never had a hamburger before, or French fries, and although they were both tasty, my stomach did not feel right after eating them. *At the end of the third day, I was given a new set of documents with American credentials, and then I was placed on a Miami-bound plane.*

During the entire flight, all that I could think about was how were Angela and the girls doing without me. *I missed them greatly, especially now being out of Cuba and so far from any possible contact with them.* I was living hell on earth, and my only redemption would be reuniting with my family. As soon as we landed in Miami, I was greeted by two new FBI agents, who cleared me through immigration. *I was then at once placed on a plane bound for Newark, New Jersey.*

Angela

I was determined to make Abuela's guava marmalade an incredibly famous and successful business for us in Pinar Del Río. Though I had limited resources, I knew, if I could produce enough, that I had many possible outlets available for selling it among the stores and shops of the city. *Raul had come by to tell us the great news of Ricardo's successful journey to America!* He asked us all to be patient and said that the plans for joining him there were in the works. He also came with a letter which Ricardo had written before having left Cuba. In it, Ricardo had professed his love and his promise to work both day and night until we were together again. At the bottom, there was a rough drawing of a map of our backyard. Ricardo had circled a spot beneath the flaming tree marked off by the length of a meter in the direction of a rose bush he and I had planted together our first month in our new home. With Raul's help, we dug and found a metal box full of money and all of our official documents. A smile came to my face since this brought me great relief. I would be able to purchase boxes of mason jars along with several large pots and spoons and a plentiful amount of sugar to get my business off the ground.

I had learned to drive with Manuela's help and had finally acquired my driver's license. Just when I was trying to decide how much money to put aside for a used automobile, which we would need to deliver the marmalade to the stores, one morning I awoke to find Ricardo's car out in our driveway once again. *I trembled at the sight.* Either it was a trick, or René had somehow found a soft spot for us. I noticed the keys were in the ignition, and yet I let the aqua blue Ford Sedan sit there untouched for two weeks. Finally, need itself helped me to overcome my doubts and worry. Getting off to a late start, the girls had missed their bus, and I started the car and drove them to school. *From then on, I used it regularly.*

Eventually, Enriqueta began coming around again and thankfully never asked a single question about Ricardo or what had happened. With the help of her two boys and my two oldest girls, we began canning mason jars full of marmalade fresh from the stove. I asked her, and she agreed right away to go into business with me. I then began receiving regular letters and packages from a Richard Russo of a city called West New York in the American state of New Jersey. The packages always contained a bit of money, vitamin supplements, coffee, dried mashed potatoes, candies of all sorts of varieties, and every flavor of gum imaginable. *Of course, this was Ricardo with our new surname and our new home.*

Even Raul and Manuela could not believe the ups and downs of our planning to rejoin Ricardo in America. My husband had petitioned congressmen from Florida and New Jersey. Ricardo had claimed us with United States Customs and Immigrations, but it did little good. He had written to governors and to the president himself. Even Raul had tried utilizing his best contacts within the

CIA. *He came by a year later to inform that all American influence had absolutely collapsed and had come to an abrupt and outright end with the failed Bay of Pigs Invasion.* I felt like we were completely on our own. *We did not know what to do or where to turn.* Nobody had given up; however, there was a feeling of listlessness and depression which suggested *we may never get to see Ricardo again.*

The girls grew, and Odalys especially loved to help me with the preparation of the fresh guavas for the marmalade. We kept busy, and we never lost hope. Ricardo began telling us in his weekly letters all about New Jersey. Where he lived, many Italian families had settled together with the large influx of Cuban exiles. He even said it reminded him somewhat of living right here in Pinar Del Río, except for the long, cold, and snowy winters. He was teaching history now at a community college and said that he loved America but could not understand its politics. His frustration over finding a way for us to get there became increasingly significant. As well, Raul had no firm answers, and during the years which followed, *it seemed more definite that it might never happen at all.* I kept busy, otherwise I would have become despondent, but I was determined not to allow Castro yet another victory over the spirit and character of the Cuban people.

As horrible as it was, we had been in Cuba without Ricardo for six long years! So frustrated had Ricardo become that on more than one occasion in his letters, he talked of coming back into Cuba with his previous assumed Uruguayan identity. *I pleaded with him not to and to have faith that all would work out.*

Then as we approached the latter part of 1966, a swell of discontent rose in Cuba, fed by economic hardship along with the erosion and virtual disappearance of political freedoms. It was painful for me when Castro closed down small businesses altogether and eliminated all private property. Many more Cubans began turning against his *revolution.* With unrest mounting quickly, Castro opened the port of Camarioca, allowing relatives from Miami to come and *collect* those left behind in Cuba. Within a few weeks thereafter, President Lyndon Johnson initiated the so-called *freedom flights.* I read all about it each morning in the newspapers, and I believed that since Ricardo had already claimed us with US Customs and Immigration, *I could travel with the girls on a flight to Miami.* I immediately called Raul, and then Manuela, Blanca, and Enriqueta, *who all agreed this is just what I had been waiting on for so long.*

I was worried of the repercussions that we might face leaving the island. I knew from reports from others that the first thing which would happen would be that our house would immediately be sealed by Castro's government, and I hated thinking that the milicianos would take over our home. However, this was a small thing. I finally told my family everything, and they could not believe it. They asked what I would do, and when I told them about the freedom flights to America, they questioned if I could leave everything behind. I told them I would miss them all immensely, but really, there was no choice. *"Yes, we will do it." Eventually, a quarter of a million Cubans would immigrate into the United States via the freedom flights initiated by the US government.*

With extraordinarily little preparation, I hugged Enriqueta, the boys, and even Paco, and then Raul drove us to Jose Marti International Airport, the same place where years earlier Ricardo had left from for freedom. Raul and Marge said their goodbyes, and I promised we would stay in touch. I knew I could never thank him enough for all he did for us all these years. My five girls all quiet and uncertain, we boarded an Eastern Airlines plane by walking out through the terminal on to the tarmac. Throughout the long and quiet flight, we could not rest easily until we finally reached Miami. *I would discover later that Ricardo had to work a second job at a factory in order to send Raul the money necessary to pay for the paperwork and flight.* The US government finally assisted us once we landed due to Raul's connections with the CIA and in gratitude for Ricardo's part long before. They picked us up from the airport and drove my five girls and me in a van for processing at the Immigration and Customs Office downtown Miami.

With our new United States credentials, *we boarded another jet later that evening, heading for Newark, New Jersey.* All the girls were extremely excited to be seeing Ricardo once again. Baby Odalys, now seven, had images in her mind of what her father had looked like the last time she had seen him in his cowboy attire as we drove by the embassy, and she talked for the entire plane ride about what he must look like now. As Ricardo had years before, we landed in Newark Airport. *I still could not believe we were actually here.* We came down the long stairway and finally into the terminal as Odalys searched the throngs of people, looking for her papo. Spotting a man who was looking directly at her with a smile upon his face, so excited to finally see her papo again, *Odalys ran right to him.* He did not know what to do as my little girl wrapped her arms around his legs. I came running over immediately and took Odalys by the hand, gently pulling her off the man, *who had in fact, not been her papo.*

Her Papo had been adjacent to where this man had been, behind a very large grouping of people who had been awaiting loved ones departing from the numerous gates. Seeing me taking Odalys into my arms, he called out, *"Angela!"* I turned immediately to see Ricardo, and my heart fainted with relief. *Once he was in my arms again, I swore I never wanted him to be away from my side ever again.* Each of the girls clung to him for minutes, and we all just stood together right there in the middle of the busy terminal, feeling for the first time in six years what it meant to have our family once again. None of us were inclined to move a single muscle.

That first night, Odalys would sleep on her papo's chest, with Natalia and Marie sprawled out on one side of him in the large king bed, and Mary and Olivia on the other. Ricardo had made sure that he had gotten the small house ready for us, everything looked great, *and I did not mind sharing our bed with our five girls in the least.*

Thereafter, we resumed our lives in the city of West New York, New Jersey—a genuinely nice town directly along the Hudson River. *New York City was always right there across the broad river, keeping a watchful eye over us.* Ten months after our reunion, our first and only boy, whom we named Ricardo Jr., would be born. Ricardo never again flew on a plane for fear of being hijacked back to Castro's rule. *He would never return to his beloved homeland, Cuba.*

Castro's Early Reign

In 1961, the Cuban government nationalized all property. They took everything held by religious organizations, including the great number of parishes, orphanages, and land owned by the Roman Catholic Church. Thousands of church members, including its bishop, were permanently expelled from the nation. Homeless children were sent to work and army camps. The new Cuban government officially then declared itself atheist. Assassinations at the wall continued unabated for more than four years. Private schools were banned, and the state assumed almost absolute control over all the country's children. The Cuban government then expropriated all assets from mafia leaders, taking large sums of cash.

In July of 1961, Fidel Castro's 26th of July Movement merged with the People's Socialist Party and the Revolutionary Directorate on the thirteenth of March to form the Integrated Revolutionary Organizations (IRO). On March 26, 1962, the IRO became the United Party of the Cuban Socialist Revolution (PURSC) which, very shortly thereafter, became the modern Communist Party of Cuba. Castro appointed himself the First Secretary of the party, remained the ruler of Cuba, and then became Cuba's first prime minister. In 1976, after having murdered thousands whom he had perceived were a threat to the authenticity of his government, he became president. Upon his retirement on February 20, 2008, his brother Raúl officially replaced him as president of Cuba.[10]

No elections were ever granted the Cuban people.

[10] https://en.wikipedia.org/wiki/Cuban_Revolution

Epilogue

Humberto Sorí Marín was extricated via a CIA established route and relocated to South Florida, where he provided valuable intelligence and was enlisted by the operative agents of the Florida Division of the Federal Bureau of Investigation (FBI).

He refused to give up his quest to free his nation of the Castro nemesis. He believed in democracy and in the Cuban constitution, but more importantly, he believed in what it was that made up the *heart of the Cuban people* more than anything else. Like Ricardo, he could not stand idly by and let Castro take that from his beloved countrymen, his culture, and his family without a fight.

The following was published by *Parade* magazine in Miami, Florida, on April 12, 1964, and had been written by columnist Andrew St. George under the title of "The Attempt to Assassinate Castro":

> It was the assassination attempt just before the Bay of Pigs that was the most significant of all. It involved several senior commanders of the Cuban Revolutionary Armed Forces as well as key civilian leaders.
>
> The Central Intelligence Agency, which had received absolutely reliable reports that a conspiracy to assassinate Castro was developing among his top lieutenants, decided to contact the plotters, because the U.S. was already training its own anti-Castro force in Guatemala. CIA agents discovered the conspiracy had a wealthy con-

tact man in Miami, a former sugar cane grower, Alberto Fernandez.

With CIA's tacit approval, Fernandez bought a converted subchaser, the *Texana III*, and had it outfitted with concealed deck armaments, 50-cal. machine guns, two 57 mm. recoilless rifles and a pair of small speedboats with muffled interceptor engines.

Now began one of the most daring and extraordinary secret intelligence operations ever attempted. Shuttling in the dark of night between Marathon Key and the north coast of Cuba, the Texana III was the link between the Cuban conspirators and the U.S.

Its two deck boats shimmered up to shore less than a dozen miles from Havana to pick up their unusual passengers: Cuban rebel comandantes in full uniform and governmental functionaries carrying briefcases.

Before the sun came up, the travelers were in U.S. waters, where they held quick conferences with American agents, sped back to Cuba the next night.

The tricky and hazardous process went on for a couple of months, and the U.S. learned more and more about the murder conspiracy beaded by cool, brainy Comandante Humberto Sorí Marín, a hero of the Castro revolution. Other top-level men involved astounded the Americans: Secret Police Chief Aldo Vera; Comandante Julio Rodriguez, deputy commandant of the San Antonio de los Banos air base; several Navy flag officers; the military superintendent of Camagüey Province; the

> president of the Cuban Sugar Institute; and the undersecretary of finance. They were determined to act early in 1961. The plot was to kill both Castros and touch off a general uprising.
>
> Convinced that, regardless of what the U.S. did, the conspirators meant business, the CIA decided to capitalize on the plot without actually participating in it. Officials readied the landing forces to go ashore at the same time. Agents began a series of secret meetings in Havana with the conspirators to coordinate their plans.[11]

Miami, April 20, 1961, by United Press International (UPI)—regarding Sorí Marín fleeing after the first attempted assassination of Castro, but then returning for yet a second.

> Sorí Marín fled in a small boat to Miami (after the December attempt) but returned about three months later to Cuba. He said he was disillusioned with feuding among anti-Castro factions and believed he could do more in Cuba....
>
> It appeared Castro had rounded up all possible leaders of an uprising and was terrorizing Cubans with new executions to keep the populace quiet. Thousands were reported jailed. Among them was Martin Houseman, the second UPI correspondent to be arrested in Havana.
>
> Despite Castro's iron grip, there was gunfire today in Havana. The Cuban radio said a girl was killed and another wounded by gunfire from a car near the intelligence service headquarters.

[11] http://www.latinamericanstudies.org/belligerence/parade.htm

> Eight persons were executed Tuesday and nine yesterday.
>
> Nearly 700 have died before Castro's firing squads since he seized power in January 1959.
>
> In the previous 58 years of Cuban history, only three persons had been legally executed.
>
> The broadcast said the men were executed for plotting to assassinate Castro.[12]

And then from a *Wikipedia* article regarding Sorí Marín:

> On the night of 13 March 1961, Sorí Marín, Rafael Diaz Hanscom, Manuel Puig Miyar, Nemesio Rodriguez Navarrete and Gaspar Domingo Trueba Varona landed from a boat at Fundora Point, Celimar, near Havana, with arms and explosives.[13]

And finally, the remainder of the *Parade* magazine story:

> Then, just before the target date, there occurred one of those impossible mistakes nobody ever believes. A crucially important secret conference was being held with most of the top conspirators. They met in a house of known safety in Havana's Miramar suburb on a tranquil street, Calle Once. It was a large, yellow, somnolent building, lived in and owned by a respectable retired sugar engineer and his wife.

---

[12] https://www.upi.com/Archives/1961/04/20/Seven-including-ex-Castroite-executed/1205884581438/

[13] https://en.wikipedia.org/wiki/Humberto_Sor%C3%AD_Marin

In the front patio, the engineer played gin rummy with his wife and led by many points. In the back of the house, the plotters gathered around a heavy refectory table covered with street maps, pinpointing the massive incendiary attack against the crowded downtown district of "Old Havana," which was to touch off the uprising. The Texana III had already shipped in hundreds of petacas.

Several blocks away, a militia security patrol stopped in front of another house, then entered to search it. A nervous woman in a back room fled from a rear door with her small daughter. She ran beneath garden walls and ducked into the rear entrance of the large yellow house of the engineer, an old friend.

The street was deserted. But one militiaman watched as she ran to the yellow house. So, under the blazing sky of a spring afternoon, in Miramar, the security unit walked down the street to that yellow house, that sleepy yellow house....

The pity of it was that the nervous woman who ran did not have to. The security police were on a routine search. She was suspected of nothing; if she had remained, nothing would have gone wrong.

The 11 key figures of the Sorí Marín conspiracy were caught in a single sweep. The four men who had been sent in by the CIA might have gotten away; they were all Cubans and carried such perfectly forged papers that two were subsequently shot under their assumed names.

But Sorí Marín had no chance whatever. As the milicianos burst into the room, his pistol leaped into his hand. But the security men's snub-nosed Czech Tommy guns chattered and Sori Martin crumpled as he tried to crash though a window.

And it was all a mistake. The militia walked in by mistake. The woman ran away by mistake.

Washington working with fragmented information, decided it was too late to halt the invasion troops staging for departure in Guatemala. There was no way to know just how badly the conspiracy had been crippled; there was a possibility that many of its members had not been identified and would thus be able to carry out the plans.

April 17, 1961, at dawn, the seven top conspirators, led by Sori Martin, wounded and supported by his guards, but still wearing his uniform, were executed in Havana. Within the next few hours, they were followed to the wall by the captured CIA men. The rest, the slaughter at the Bay of Pigs, is history.

U.S. security and intelligence agencies are now more worried about the possibility of a successful assassination. For Washington-which once gave tacit support to Sori Marin-now feels that a real explosion involving Castro could trigger the most unpredictable chain reaction of the coming year, a chain reaction that conceivably could turn into World War III.[14]

[14] http://www.latinamericanstudies.org/belligerence/parade.htm

References

Communications Editors—The Central Intelligence Agency. 1963. *The Initial Aims of the 26th of July Movement.* Approved For Release 2004/06/24: CIA-RDR79T00429A001400010010-0, Washington, DC: The CIA.

Editors of *Encyclopedia Britannica.* 2020. "Cuba Cultural Institutions." February. Accessed June 3, 2020. https://www.britannica.com/place/Cuba/Cultural-institutions.

St. George, Andrew. 1964. "The Attempt to Assassinate Castro." *Parade Magazine* (April): 3–7.

The Editorial Staff at *Wikipedia.* 2020. "The Cuban Revolution." June 7. Accessed June 23, 2020. https://en.wikipedia.org/wiki/Cuban_Revolution.

—.2020. *Wikipedia.* "Cuba During World War II." May 24. Accessed May 30, 2020. https://en.wikipedia.org/wiki/Cuba_during_World_War_II.

The Editorial Staff of *Wikipedia.* 2020. "Humberto Sorí Marín." May 5. Accessed June 30, 2020. https://en.wikipedia.org/wiki/Humberto_Sor%C3%AD_Marin.

UPI Editors and Writers. 1961. *UPI Archives.* "Seven including ex-Castroite executed." Accessed May 9, 2020. https://www.upi.com/Archives/1961/04/20/Seven-including-ex-Castroite-executed/1205884581438/.

CPSIA information can be obtained
at www.ICGtesting.com
Printed in the USA
LVHW030600190121
676854LV00004B/287